How to Become a Better Person:

25 Ways to Improve Your Life

Sage Egerton

DEDICATION

To my loving and amazing family

CONTENTS

ACKNOWLEDGMENTS

This work would not have been possible without the support and love from my family, who have always believed in me and pushed me to pursue my dreams. Thank you, and love you, always.

1 APPRECIATION

There Is Simply No Room for Negativity to Creep into a Grateful Heart

Become a better person by being thankful. As simple as that sounds, it is difficult to be always be grateful when hardships and struggles seem to be lurking in every corner of your life (on the other hand, life is never a perfect circle but rather a bizarre quasi-circle with a multitude of edges and spikes that may look like a circle from afar; therefore, life never rolls easily). You will never become a better person by expecting the world to love you while doing nothing. You have to love the world first, and only then the world will start to love you back. The so-called karma is not confined just between persons. Gratefulness cycles through actions and words. Being thankful one day leads to more days of appreciation. Because there is simply no room for negativity to creep into a grateful heart, everyday will feel like a gift once you start appreciating everything and anything life throws at you, be it people or Mondays.

Compliment, Not Complain

Be thankful for the smallest and most unlikely reasons. If you look closely, the world is actually full of appreciative, appreciable moments and occasions. Because to appreciate something depends on the mind and not on the situation, the same circumstances can be felt differently for everyone. Sunny days call for picnics, and hot teas taste better on cloudy days. A congested traffic lets you listen to your favorite songs longer, and long day at work makes you appreciate coming home more than anything. Poor examples, maybe, but you get the idea. All it takes is your willingness and change of perspective. You can celebrate anything and everything, any day and everyday if you choose. We are already adept at spotting faults and flaws in the only good things we have going, so why not reverse the attitude and work on it? Compliment, not complain.

Understandably, sometimes you may feel as if certain stressful stimuli are impossible to swallow and ignore. However, to express stress outwardly is not always the best method to relieve stress. More often than not, expressing anger and frustration makes you aware of the stressful situation more vividly and, as a result, aggravates the ongoing negativity. Again, a change in perspective is what I recommend in place of raging out. Start by practicing where you try to perceive every situation in a positive light. For every darkness, there is light. Shadows form because of a light source shining down somewhere above. If something upsets you, take it as a fodder for you to grow more mature and experienced. For example, a disagreeable person in your way is not to be hated but avoided, not just for now but make the instance a teaching moment for you to spot and shun the similarly toxic, distasteful individuals pop up in your life forever and whenever. If you end up getting hurt from relationships, make your history your textbook and learn to meet people more carefully. If your mistakes made you miserable, make sure you do not make the same mistakes again. There is a positive in the utmost negative of persons, things, and events. You just have to learn how to discern and take advantage of such teaching moments. That is how you become a better person as you strive forward. Never despair some awfulness happened, appreciate that it happened for you to learn and grow.

To Appreciate Is a Continuous, Lifelong Action

Be grateful for what you have right now. You have many things at your side in case you have not noticed. How about your family, friends, and lovers for starters? What about your health, educational background to read and write, mental capacity to want to become better and have a better life (and a little naivete that has led you to read my writing, thank you very much)? Of course, you have more things that you do not have than you do have. But do understand that you will not and cannot have everything life. You simply cannot have everything in life. No one can. But you do have enough things in your life for which to be thankful one by one, and it is for certain that you will still run out of time before you fully appreciate them all. Can you ever be completely grateful for your parents' love, your friends' support, and your lovers' presence in your lifetime? Is such a feat even possible? The answer is, 'what matters and matters alone is you start now and appreciate them truly to the end of time To appreciate is a continuous, lifelong action that never ends because the target of your appreciation also keeps growing. There will come more things to be grateful as you live. So rest assured as you will never run out of things to be thankful and spread love and thanks all around.

Be Grateful That Today Has Been a Better Day Than Yesterday

Ask yourself whether you are taking too much of too many things for granted. If you think you can find nothing in your life for which you can be grateful, it is most likely that you are not looking properly. Perhaps you think all the luxuries you are enjoying are free and that you deserve every one of them all on your account. When and if you feel such a way in any time in your life, just remember that you are but a part of history. For instance, imagine a world without air conditioner. Imagine a world without internet connection, without any concept of written language, a proper sewer system, electricity, and—here comes the most devastating loss of human history—Instagram. Jokes aside, what most and many unfortunate, unhappy people make mistakes at is that they believe they are entitled to the world's gifts geniuses. Do note that no one has earned the rights to enjoy the civilization's inventions and provisions. We are all just benefiting as naturally and freely as we breathe in air (but at the current rate of environmental destruction the metaphor will soon have to be updated). We should never compare ourselves with other people with seemingly more wealth and fortune in their favors. To be honest, that seems to be the definition of comparison nowadays, not to mention the definition of unhappiness. We feel robbed and deprived when nothing is taken away from us when we look at the more fortunate, well-to-do peers. When we look around others for comparison, we become blind to what we already have, as well as dull our sense of appreciation and gratitude. The only comparisons we should make to make ourselves happier and progressive are the ones made against the past of both the universal and the personal history. Be grateful that today has been a better day than yesterday, or a century ago. Block out other people enjoying their present moments. Instead, focus on your own life, and you start by be thankful for what you have.

Appreciation Is Contagious

Start thanking, and soon the thanks come back to you. Appreciation, or gratitude, is contagious. The thankful people will soon surround themselves with like-minded thankers due to the simple fact that they are just so likeable. People want to be around those who make them feel better. On the contrary, no one wants to be near whiners and complainers. You must agree that life is too short to put up with those negative people anyway. It is your choice: you can be one of those feel-good people with a simple attitude change, a slight tweak to your perspective of the world and yourself, along with a few words of genuine gratefulness from your heart, or else. Besides, nothing bad has ever come out from situations ending with "thank you's" (unless sarcasm was involved and the thank was not genuine, and even then a little twisted humor is preferable to straight whining, I think; a joker whines and complains in style, at least). Usually, a smile or a "you're welcome" follows an expression of gratitude and appreciation. With enough smiles and exchange of niceties, the world could become a better place one day. But your world, and the bettered yourself, can come earlier and easier, and it is all on you. Try and see how a 'thank you' and a returned smile can make your day. Days make up a life eventually, after all.

2 COMPASSION

There Seems to Be More Evil Than Good in This World

How to be compassionate may be easier to explain than why. The world is no doubt an evil, cruel place filled with like-minded inhabitants all around, and you may ask yourself why you should be kind when everyone else is, or at least appears to be, not. Everywhere you look around, there seems to be more evil than good on this planet we have no choice but to call 'home.' The "how's" of compassion—namely being kind, harming none, helping others, and other saintly acts and reservations—seem utterly futile and meaningless against the prevalent evil and callousness that have plagued this world and the humanity for centuries and continuing.

The aggravating problem is that it appears as if being selfish and immoral is more beneficial than being altruistic and ethical at times. The good and the kind, in turn, are often victimized and disadvantaged rather than celebrated and respected as they should rightfully be. Surely, it is not for honor or recognition that we should try to become kind and compassionate. It is for the better of the self and ultimately the entire world that compassion should be fostered and practiced in everyone's life. The only catch is that compassion is rarely conspicuous and often overlooked in place of a more direct, immediately rewarding behaviors and attitudes such as belligerence and selfishness. We know all too well that revenge is oh-so-sweet, and there is never enough pie to share around with everyone. I truly want to say that compassion prevails in the end, but we have witnessed too many accounts too many times where compassion is laid to waste and the evil, lesser or absolute, go unpunished and even victorious.

Only If Everyone Were Kind and Compassionate Towards One Another

Compassion is a virtue that not everyone can have. It is almost like a talent or a gift, for to be compassionate all the time does require more than just willingness and general love for the world. But imagine what a world we could be living right now if everyone were kind and compassionate towards one another. Unfortunately, the ever so diligent balance of nature simply does not allow the good to outnumber the bad at any point of time. The opposite of that, however, does not seem to hold true, as our fallible human minds recognize the bad more clearly and sensitively than we recognize the good and, therefore, perceive the bad and the evil to outnumber their benign counterparts. Regardless of whether such a perception is objectively true or subjectively biased (hint: it is the latter), we are indeed exposed and more readily responsive towards the negative stimuli of this world. On top of that is the fact that we seek to defend ourselves foremost and at all cost, even if such a defense means inflicting offense on the other. We may never tell ourselves that we are willing and ready to hurt and harm others just for the sake of hurting and harming, but the truth, and what matters, is that we are capable of damage and harm when it comes to protecting ourselves and our loved ones. Compassion, of course, does not extend beyond the impossible demand of unconditional sacrifice or outright surrender of our causes. Yet to conveniently deem compassion as a variable, circumstantial kindness is a bit irresponsible, if not erroneous.

Is Universal Compassion Truly Impossible?

Perhaps compassion is still too early for the humankind, whose history of war, discrimination, murder, and hatred is an ongoing schedule to date. Despite belonging to the same species, humans display arrays of personalities and preferences that make compassionate, altruistic efforts only one-sided. Some people are more inclined towards being compassionate while others exhibit evil more easily and evidently. The trend seems to continue in the future as well. Neither natural selection nor evolutionary process conclusively favors the kind over the evil, meaning that the strong and the powerful that survive throughout generations may continue to be an ambivalent mix of the good and the evil. The genes and the cultures passed down from the victors, benevolent or baneful, will shape the humanity in both directions with equal success and failure. Unless a drastic change occurs to alter the human nature to be uniform and indistinct, the humanity may be doomed for eternity in terms of never being a perfectly kind and altruistic species. Not only is the humankind unready to be completely compassionate, but it may as well be impossible by design to acquire such a state of being.

We Are Susceptible to Evil

We may never be completely and universally compassionate, but we should not stop trying. One of the most humanly human flaws is the relative easiness and naturalness of committing evil than performing good. For instance, a child instinctively knows and learns to lie even without having anyone teaching or advising to practice the said vice. The same can be said about violence, greed, and jealousy, all of which are often observable in even the most innocent of us. Virtues, on the other hand, are not only difficult to achieve but also fragile to keep developing as one negative enforcement discourages from further practices. For example, a child who benefits from lying and deceiving may continue to do so until corrected otherwise or suffering from the consequences. In both cases of continuation and termination, feedback is apparent and direct. Virtues, however, take a longer time to receive a feedback. A good deed often goes unnoticed and unappreciated. An honest child should be recognized and praised, but rather we expect children to be innocent and flawless while taking their purity for granted only to be shocked when they are just smaller versions of us. As a result, we are conditioned and enforced from childhood to get by with a vice or two here and there.

Despite our innate proclivity to evil, and even because of the designed flaw in ourselves, we should consciously and conscientiously strive to better ourselves and be virtuous. Even with all our efforts to become good, the best and the most optimal we can reach is the half-way point between the evil and the good. Compassion is just one example to fight against our natural urge to indulge in evil conveniently. Compassion also encompasses many virtues into one. We act kindly and understand differences amongst ourselves when we are being actively and deliberately compassionate. Compassion may as well be just for show, as the phrase 'show compassion' implies, and perhaps all we can do is to cover up our inner evil by putting on a show. Nonetheless, to realize and acknowledge that we are susceptible to evil is a start of improvement. Showing compassion may not mean much in the broader context of the inherently evil humanity. But for now, we do what we can.

3 CONFIDENCE

Being Humble Is Not Equivalent to Lacking Confidence

Confidence is generally good. Sometimes too much confidence can hurt you, but it is often the lack of confidence that causes problems. To note, being humble is not equivalent to lacking confidence. Some people like to see humility and modesty in others while some like to be around confident, purposeful people. No one, however, likes people who are meek and uncertain about themselves. In fact, even though humility seems and feels like the polar opposite of confidence, they are actually complements to one another. Being humble without the inner confidence is just obsequiousness. The truth is that you can lower yourself down only when you have the ability to lift yourself up anytime you want. In a way, only the truly confident can be humble, and humility comes from confidence.

There Is Always the Optimal Middle-Ground in Everything

To find the optimal point between overconfidence and humbleness is the key, and that key comes through being reticent. Overconfidence is just distasteful while being too humble may come across as groveling and even mocking at times. Therefore, the best strategy to situate yourself in the middle-ground of optimal confidence is to talk less. Talking leads to a lot of mistakes, including boasting, exaggerating, and lying among others, while showing through action is authentic and apparent. You cannot be a braggart if you keep your mouth shut from showing off what you have or do not have. Most of our relationship problems comes from either blabbering away too much or not talking at all. Extremes are bad, and there is always the optimal middle-ground in everything.

Confidence Is the Fuel That Your Will Burns and Consumes

Confidence is the gasoline while you are still the vehicle that is running and running in your life. Confidence is only an accessory that you can manage to live without if you really have to, however incomplete and miserable such a life will be. Just as an automobile is useless if it sits in the garage collecting dust, your life cannot find its meaning if it is not moving forward. Confidence is the fuel that your will burns and consumes to drive itself. Just as you eat breakfast to start your day and lunch to keep your day going, you may even consider preparing confidence boosters throughout your day on a regular basis. For example, lunchtime usually marks the halfway point of a day, and you should come up with a routine to look back the prior morning to find any occasion to boost your confidence to last your latter half of the day. In my case, I always write my daily quota in the morning, and I tell myself to be proud of whatever garbage of a writing that I have written (and that you are reading) as I stuff a couple hot dogs or fifty-cents-a-cup noodles into my mouth at lunch. Hey, a little confidence is better than no confidence after all.

Confidence cannot be everything but it can help with everything. Confidence may come across as a luxury for some people who have never had it nor benefited from it in their lives. Understandably, confidence can backfire on a person when things go wrong, and sometimes it is better to stay low-key and inconspicuous than be flashy and garnering attentions unnecessarily. I cannot speak for every individual life and history in which whether confidence or absence of it has helped more; to each person his or her choice of living. What I can speak for, however, is that confidence indubitably helps those who want to achieve and have a better tomorrow. Being confident may draw in unwanted enemies who want you to fail and curious eyes that will watch your every move and action with callous indifference. But it is not to prove the doubters and haters wrong but to make your life more interesting, energetic, and progressive; it is solely for your sake that you should be confident no matter who says no and what situations challenge you. The analogy still stands: it is up to you to feed whether cheap or premium gasoline (i.e. the sense of living just for the sake of not dying or the positive confidence that wills your life towards great things, respectively) to your most valuable vehicle (i.e. yourself).

We Cannot Be Imperfect Perfectly and Completely

You can be confident of anything and for any reason. Just as you can find joy in the smallest delights this world offers, you can take pride in and be confident of anything and everything you possess. Thanks to our humanly imperfections, we do and always will have two sides of everything, albeit in a flawed, inadequate manner. While we cannot be perfect in all aspects, we cannot be imperfect perfectly and completely. Everyone has a weakness and a strength, often but not necessarily polar opposites of each other. We may be mediocre in some aspects, but such is the norm and considerably better than being completely incompetent in all areas. It is still up to us to find our strengths and hone those merits while trying to make up for our weaknesses and flaws. Let us be humble that we are not perfect and yet take pride in what we excel at, however few or subjectively insignificant they may be.

Confidence Should Be Lit in Only One Place: Your Heart

Confidence is the fire burning within, while humility is the light that glows outwardly. You do not want to touch the fire, nor do you want others get burned from it. Thus, you keep the confidence burning and keeping you warm only on the inside. You do not even have to show your confidence towards others as you are the only designated recipient of the fiery confidence. What others should see is the glow that flows out of you and maybe feel the slightest touch of warmth from witnessing your energetic, passionate actions in life. Visualize yourself as either a cozy fireplace or a glass lamp. The fireplace never leaves its post and instead burns steadily and quietly while fulfilling its purpose of keeping the house warm sturdily and infallibly. A glass lamp lights the dark streets or the paths ahead of the beholder as it lights up efficiently and safely enclosed in a clear, transparent glass case. Confidence should be lit in only one place, and that is your heart. You should be focused on keeping the confidence alive and make it an engine to serve your purpose while other extraneous perks and benefits that others may receive in your vicinity should not matter to you. Fire's sole purpose is to burn. The warmth and the light are uses that the wielder of fire can exploit. Confidence is like fire, and we, the humans, are the only creatures on earth that can use fire to our advantage willingly and adeptly. Other animals may be confident of their claws, feathers, and skills, but I am sure that only we can understand the analogy of confidence and fire to burn without burning, glow without light. In fact, I am confident about it.

4 EMPATHY

The Perfectly Balanced Empathy Exists

Having too much of empathy is just as bad as having too little of it. Too much empathy just wears you out emotionally. Too little empathy, on the other hand, makes your life difficult as you are most likely friendless and lonely most of the time, unless you are perfectly fine living alone and peacefully in exchange for the warmth and fun that company provides. The good news is that there exists the middle-ground, an optimal level of being empathetic that works best for your social lives and relationships. The optimization of empathy is just another word for finding balance between concentrating on yourself and having interest in the people and the world around you. This essay will explore the ways, and why's, of finding the said perfect balance.

The Switch Theory

I have a theory regarding the optimization of empathy, and it is called the 'switch theory.' As the name suggests, the switch theory is about turning your empathy capability on or off depending on the circumstances. The switch theory is a solution to optimizing your empathy level at any given time. In its core, the switch theory is all about concentration and compromising; you concentrate on the people who need your attention and empathy the most while compromising to ignore those that do not deserve your time and care. Despite coming off as cold and callous, the reality is that your time is precious and finite as well as your energy and feelings. There is simply no time or reason for you to waste your empathy and care for those who do not appreciate you. Life is short as is for you to spend time with and enjoy the company of those whom you love. Turn your empathy switch off to any irrelevant, unpleasant people. There is no need for you to waste your time and energy on everyone and everything on this world. Be smart before being empathetic.

Do We Really Need Empathy in Our Lives?

The truth is that you can live without empathy, probably. Such a life will be lonely and boring without people loving and understanding you back, but you can still eat, sleep, and exist while food tastes less delicious and sleep only comes as a retreat from the reality. Yet some people may prefer to live without ever having to be empathetic towards others, a life without the drama and the hassle of relationships complicating their personal interests and inner peace. A solitary life is a simple life, albeit sardonic and sad at times. If you are such a person, then empathy may truly be a luxury that you will never need or want. However, even if you can live without empathy or those towards whom you feel empathetic, the fact that missing empathy in life makes you and your life incomplete and unconventional. Incompleteness and unconventionality are not necessarily bad things, but they are liabilities that may pose dangers and threats later on purely based on the society's convenience geared towards the majority and the statistical rule of the general outcomes. If you are an outlier that deviates from the norm, your life differs that much from what people deem normal. Normality and familiarity are likened to safety and reliability, and missing either safety or reliability is never a good thing in sustaining a life.

The Handkerchief Analogy

Empathy is like a handkerchief you offer to only those in need. To those in distress or mess, a handkerchief is a useful, timely tool to be appreciated and utilized. To anyone else, it is just a cloth, or maybe a silk, thrown at his or her face uncalled for and unasked for. Meanwhile, the cost of offering a handkerchief is exerted on you, be it washing it after use or never getting it back in some cases. The return over your investment may even be as small as a whispered 'thank you,' but most people do not extend help to be appreciated and thanked, but, rather, they just do it.

To liken empathy with a handkerchief or a switch that can be turned on and off may sound absurd, but in its core human emotions are all absurd, volatile, and capricious. We are often mad over the silliest reasons, happy for a short time, have different points and preferences to be joyous, passionate, and in love, and most of the time we do not have control over what and whom we like or hate. To believe that we have some control over our feelings as if we would give out handkerchiefs or manipulate a switch is not an attempt at revolutionizing how we think, feel, and live but, instead, an endeavor to give us a sense of control and confidence that we are indeed the owner and the master of our emotions and life. Most people do not carry handkerchiefs with them nowadays. Manual light switches coexist with voice activated and movement sensor versions in even the most modest modern households. Changes are being made to the culture and the technology all the time, constantly and continuously. Why not make changes in your perspective, in your own life?

Empathy Not for Utility, but for Utopia

In today's individualistic, competitive world, no one will accuse you of being apathetic and callous, at least not publicly. The world is full of such selfish, disinterested people and even acknowledges them as the efficient leaders and models of the society. The community-based world of friendly neighbors and family-oriented lifestyles has transformed into a globalized and independent world of possibilities and celebrations of the self. People no longer require an entire village's production to survive; mega-companies and distribution logistics have taken care much of our needs and necessities such as convenient acquirement of food, clothing, and even housing. Along with the convenient lifestyle came alienation and exclusivity that, in turn, has led to the restless, wary world without trust and dependence that we live today. In other words, we have exchanged comfort of life for the comfort of company. Whether it is a fair exchange or a bigger loss than gain for the entirety of the humanity is debatable. What I can tell you, however, is that a natural, and neutral, change has occurred and affected the lives of billions in the past century or so, but we as individuals still have a choice in the matter of how we want to live and with whom we want to live. Empathy is one of such choices; being empathetic may not turn you into a better person overnight, or ever, but we need it to make this world a better, livable place nonetheless.

5 FAILURE

Failure as a Revelation

Failure is a revelation. Through failing, you are aware of your deficiencies and inadequacies. That is not to say that failure is the only method of self-reflection, nor can you make failure any less painful by viewing it as a constructive, teaching moment. Yet we may as well take the situation to our advantage and turn failure into something useful for ourselves. We must not fail to take advantage of failures that happen regularly and inevitably in our lives. You may fail at everything, given that you will bounce back right away, but never at failing to seize the opportunity to learn from failures.

Failure as a Learning Opportunity

People fail all the time. Even when we are keen to notice, and be envious of, only the successful and the happy around us, the common sense tells us that there are more failures than successes in this world. We can refer to none other than our very own experience with failures and successes as the evidence. There are maybe a handful of occasions that you would regard successful over the span of your life so far while you have long stopped counting how may failures you have accrued during the same period of time. Some would say look only on the bright side and let go of the past that disagrees with you, but I disagree on such an advice. To forget a failed past means to lose a learning opportunity. To refuse to learn from mistakes and failures is to give up on having a better, progressive life ahead of you.

Take comfort that everyone else fails too. Be relieved that no one is perfect and that even the best of us make mistakes here and then. Do not stop there, however, and remember that the few who succeed in the end succeeded only because they have not given up after failing. Success is often just an improved result of a failure. We should build, not dwell, on failures. Even if you think you know this in your head, it takes courage and confidence in yourself to actually stand on the failures and use them as stepping stones towards the top. What does not kill you only makes you stronger, as one legendary German philosopher said. As long as you do not let failure end your life, there is only one direction for your life to head after hitting the rock-bottom: up.

The Danger of Young Success and Misleading Luck

Although most people would want to be successful and comfortable while they are still young, achieving success too early a stage in your life is detrimental. It becomes more dangerous when the young success is the product pure luck and nothing else much. Success in general owes a lot for its birth to luck. Newton's famous bonk in the head by an apple that led to the discovery of gravity is a famous, or even fabricated, story that teaches us that even a genius has to take a break under the tree to be brilliant. Of course, an apple hitting anyone else's head would have resulted in nothing but a couple curse words and vicious biting on the apple, as Newton's gifted mind and constant curiosity towards the natural laws and makings of the world made everything possible with the right push. The moral of the story still stands, however, that you cannot await idly for luck to come across you without any preparation. You have to be ready for luck to become success, and preparations require numerous failures to remain as failures until the right time and fortune find you.

Luck, or rather its abrupt absence, is the chief culprit that destroys a suddenly successful person. Luck comes and goes without any pattern or sign. Success built on luck can easily go away when the luck that has made it all possible vanishes without a warning. Against the arbitrary, accidental occurrence of luck and chance, all we can do is wait for luck to find us at the right timing. Until then, failures will pile up inevitably. Failing is something we can do over and over but luck is beyond our control. However shorthanded, we make do with what we are given and control what we can. Failing is literally preparing for success.

Failure > Stagnancy

Failure is an evidence that you have at least tried to do something. Failing at something is better than doing nothing at all. Surely, not doing anything prevents you from failing at anything. If 'Do nothing, fail nothing,' approach pleases you, then, by all means, do nothing for the sake of not failing. This may sound profound and welcoming to the tired, timid readers out there, but there is nothing of substance in such an attitude. This is nothing more than a temporary fix and a stance to your problems and difficulties. If you find yourself weary and wary of failing time after time, stop whatever you are doing and give yourself a break. That is, until you recover your true, confident self and ready to go onto failing again. There is simply no other choice when it comes to moving forward and keep failing. That is the only way, the true path to success.

Keep Failing, Keep Going

Failure in itself is a negative aspect in life, but a total package of failure, perseverance, and reflection bundled together is the recipe for success. To never give up after a failure is a virtue. To persevere is to succeed, as life is a game of chance and recurrence; you either give up early or live long enough to become increasingly better and ultimately win it all. Perseverance alone, however, is not enough. If you keep failing for the same reasons and for the same inadequacies, it could mean that you are too eager to get on a treadmill without fixing the fundamental problems. This is where reflection comes into play, to let you recognize and diagnose the problems that need corrections. Keep the package intact and apply each concept thoroughly, and hopefully one day life will gift you with a bit of luck that will be the success you have dreamed to achieve.

Just remember failure is never over even after a success. It is an indispensable part of our life that is both infuriating and invaluable, so befriend it, familiarize yourself and get used to it for your own good. Failure is not your enemy but your ally, a crutch rather than a curb. Master failure to become the master of life. Fail at everything but at failing to learn from failures. Failing is only a process, not the end of the world.

6 HEALTHINESS

Strong Body Births Strong Mind

Our minds are not as strong as we believe them
to be. In fact, they are as strong only as our
bodies allow them to be. As you grow older, you
get closer to this undeniable truth. The truth
hits us hard the moment we are no longer
considered young, when the seemingly endless
energy that youth has provided for us is present
no more. When you are taken down with even a
simple cold, suddenly every joy in life is sapped
away, and you desire nothing else but to get
better and live normally. No person enjoys
being sick, and we are designed in such a way
that sickness affects both our bodies and minds
alike, simultaneously. More often than not,
however, it is the bodily discomfort affecting
our moods and emotions rather than the other
way around. Something as trivial as a muscle

ache irks and irritates us while a mild letdown or a disappointment rarely hurts us physically. A heartache is more of a literary, imagined symptom than the actual heart taking a hit from a shock or sadness. One's heart rate may go up due to hormonal spikes and such, but the heart can withstand a few minutes of extra thumping unless a blood vessel is clogged somewhere as a result of the lifelong history of fatty foods and nonexistent exercise—and genes, but that is just an unlucky case. Thus, whereas mediocre minds can be gifted with strong bodies through genetic fortunes, the strong minds cannot be sustained with mediocre subpar bodies. It is not a matter of strong minds deserving strong bodies but rather a correlation between mind and body in a way that body influences the mind more than the mind affecting the body in the most general sense. What the mind can do, however, is to will one's self to become and maintain being healthy. You can never be really happy with a sick, weakened body, and even those with inborn, accidental disabilities try their best to be healthy in their own ways to ensure happiness and broaden the possibility of their lives. Such an endeavor is not only admirable but imperative for everyone, as it is to neglect and overlook health for other seemingly pressing and immediate concerns in this world.

The Starting Point of Everything

A healthy body is the foundation of all things that are possible as well as the vehicle that executes all. Without our physical bodies, not much can be done with just our minds. Even the most basic activities of life—such as eating, sleeping, and walking—require you to a functioning body at the very least. In fact, the mind's supposedly exclusive monopoly on thinking is also susceptible to bodily discomforts and distractions as you cannot think straight when you are hungry, sleepy, and confined to one place for too long. Loss of appetite comes with being sick in most cases, and insomnia is a crime committed by the mind's distress abetted by the brain, literally the head of our body, failing to regulate proper hormones and signals to end up turning our bedtime into a conscious nightmare. Some people hate walking and prefer to drive around and even not move at all until they realize what privilege it has been to walk with own legs and feet come old age and every imaginable degradation of the bones, muscles, and ligaments. Taking away the simple activities like eating, sleeping, and walking from life is not a simple subtraction of such aspects from a given life; it is all or nothing when it comes to body's capabilities and indispensability of ensuring a functioning life, let alone a happy, fulfilling one.

Spoiler Alert: We All Die at One Point or Another

Health deteriorates, naturally. No one can be healthy forever no matter how hard one tries. Age is the chief culprit to our declining bodies, and the polluted, contaminated world in which we live does not help our cause to remain strong and healthy. That does not mean, however, that such an attempt is futile. In spite of the dooming future, and even because we are up against tremendous odds, we should actively try to maintain and improve our health against the toxins to which we are exposed as well as the natural aging and death of our cells. Without a̶ ̶ ̶ ̶mpt at staying healthy, we fail inevi̶ ̶ ̶ ̶se, we all die eventually one way ̶ ̶ ̶ we can at least choose how we live̶ ̶ ̶e comes. We will surren̶ ̶ ̶r disease that takes us down at̶ ̶ ̶stantly attacked by death's b̶ ̶ ̶ents and tragedies. Whether ̶ ̶ ̶ and easily to all the threats to ̶ ̶ ̶ght against to save ourselves ev̶ ̶ ̶nts of comfort and happiness is̶ ̶ ̶cide. Some would say there is a̶ ̶ ̶he fight against any unbeatable foe̶ ̶ ̶ in this case, especially when̶ ̶ ̶high as our own health and well-̶ ̶ ̶rest of our lives.

Quality, Not Quantity

Stay healthy not for longevity, but for the quality of life. Some brave and audacious people proudly claim to be fine living shortly and dying young in exchange for enjoying wanton pleasures and reckless debaucheries of the world. After all, they would argue, life is short and death is inevitable, so why not enjoy anything and everything while we still can? To counter this hedonistic argument, one must remember that most sensual pleasures, chiefly sex, alcohol, and drugs, ruin health fast and surely with repeated, unchecked exploitation. An hour of pleasure granted by substances and irresponsibility boomerangs back with a lifetime of ailments, regrets, and irrevocable damages.

A Difficult Path

Eat with caution, drink less, sleep plentifully, and exercise regularly. A simple regimen, indeed, but many people struggle to keep up with it. When it comes to being healthy, it is often moderation and self-control that are required rather than forceful changes and drastic measures. The same can be said about the overall effort to bettering the self. You do not become healthy overnight nor do you become a better person after reading a few essays urging you to become one. Both healthiness and becoming a better person require time, patience, and steady effort to maintain the desired state of being. To live such a way is by no means an easy path to take in a life. It is, however, a worthy challenge and a beneficial undertaking in long-term. We are talking about your health and life, after all, and as to what else comes before your health and life, I fail to come up with an answer.

7 HONESTY

Honesty Always Prevails

Honesty always wins in the end. Lying and running away from a problem are only temporary fixes that eventually come to haunt you. Even when it seems as if you are making things look bad by being honest at the present, it is better to be bad now than be increasingly worse in the future. Lies and wrongdoings become more unforgivable with each passing time. In the meantime, your conscience and soul are being crushed from the pressure and apprehension of being exposed.

When we are honest, we should not expect to be forgiven or condoned easily. The issuance of forgiveness and pardons for our wrongdoings are beyond our control and never up to us. What is up to us and within our control, however, is our decision to be honest at all times. That decision, in turn, gives us a sense of control and confidence to deal with problems that are often dealt with lies and deceptions in the worst alternative cases. Forgiveness or not, the empowerment of control and confidence through honesty alone should encourage everyone to choose honesty over deceit and become a truthful, responsible person as a result.

Self-Honesty

The best kind of honesty is being honest with yourself. Only by being truly honest with your actions and mind can you be honest towards others as well. Being honest is not just about refraining from lying and deceiving but also about being confident and owning up your actions and words. In fact, you have to be confident and responsible to prevail against the seemingly convenient, easy route of lying yourself out of trouble. Being honest with yourself also includes being straightforward with your needs and wants and not excusing yourself from blame arbitrarily. You cannot make exceptions and excuses for actions and behaviors that should be corrected and abstained from anyone, and that includes yourself too.

Lying Is for the Weak

We lie because we feel weak. We lie to get out of the moment where we have lost control and feel insecure. Instead of running away, we should train ourselves to face the problem and be honest. By being honest, you are taking control and being responsible for what seems to be slipping away from your hands. Bygones be bygones, and you have to concern yourself less with what has happened and more with how you will own up your mistakes. Being honest empowers you. Remember that you can be in control anytime you want. All it takes is a little courage and understanding that you are doing yourself a long-term favor by being truthful all the time.

The Truth About "White Lies"

The so-called 'white lies' are products of consideration rather than dishonesty. I personally do not oppose bending the truth a little to assuage the impact on the bearer who can be emotionally vulnerable at the moment to take in the actual, often brutal truth. The only caution is to not twist the truth too drastically. The white lie has to have a resemblance of the original truth that it is trying to cover up to minimize the damage. For example, breaking the news of a loved one's death should at least include the information that the said loved one will be missing for a long time and at least not in a foreseeable future, hopefully until the truth can be taken in full front. More importantly, the white lies have to be told in good faith and will and never for selfish reasons. To snidely turn a lie to save one's face into a white lie that supposedly benefits the weaker and the vulnerable is just another deception, if not more condemnable than any other.

No Lie Lasts Forever

No one likes liars, and no liar is perfect to keep up with his or her lies forever. The truth always comes out and the liars and the deceivers are punished not only eventually but constantly, with their conscience and nerves hurting from maintaining the falsehood from falling. On the other hand, everyone loves an honest person. Moreover, we can be honest all the time without failing and being afraid to be revealed as who we really are. In fact, honesty shows who we are, if not the best we can be. The difficult part about being honest, to muster the courage and decide to become a better person, only lasts a second while the consequence of lying torments you for day, years, and more.

Being honest becomes easier once the streak goes and you establish yourself as an honest person. Once you realize that honesty is the best policy, being honest becomes a second nature. Understandably, lying feels and comes out like a true second nature for most people. We are indubitably prone to vices and taking easy roads rather than being strict with ourselves by upholding virtues and taking the rough roads. Besides, one may ask how damaging can one lie or a deceitful act can be, while also claiming that a liar or a deceiver does not automatically become an evil person. The fact is we are natural liars. We lie because lying is one way to solve problems, if not the best way in some cases. To hold us accountable for every lie and deem us inherently evil is wrong. Yet while we are not necessarily evil when we lie and deceive, we certainly are not better than when we are honest and responsible. By lying and being dishonest, we rob ourselves of chances to become better, if not the best that we can be.

The choice is yours, of course. But if you are reading this book, I assume and hope that you have an intent to better yourself. The perks of being honest are numerous, as listed on this essay, but the best benefit in terms of improving the self is that honesty is the foundation on which other, further improvements can be made. Being honest is, in short, taking the more difficult path when an easier option is available. It is easy to just let life flow and we do absolutely nothing to change the world around us and even ourselves, but—because we can and we want to—some of us dream of becoming better people, of having better tomorrow than yesterday, and gladly take the harder road, honestly and earnestly.

8 HUMILITY

The Appeals of Humility

Everyone loves a humble person. A humble person shows through not words but actions alone. A humble person never lies or exaggerates. A humble person is respectful and considerate in dealing with others. A humble person... you get the idea. What is there not to like about a humble person? I cannot come up with a single flaw in being humble, a character that is a combination of many other virtues such as maturity, patience, broad-mindedness, and so forth.

More often than not, humility is a sign of greatness. Only those who have achieved greatness and reached the top can be truly humble. That does not mean, however, that only the great people can be humble. Greatness is not a prerequisite for being humble, nor is it a factor in any way. The correlation exists, nonetheless, and is worthy of note. Between being great and being humble, the latter is more accessible and easier to start. To maintain a true, authentic humility is a whole new different challenge, but starting the habit of humbling yourself and resist condescension is only a matter of a slight attitudinal tweak. Greatness will find the humble mind sooner or later. In fact, greatness without humility is incomplete. Greatness will be recognized in full only when the great exhibit true and admirable humility alongside.

The Danger of Fake Humility

Being too humble can be unpleasant at times. When credit is due, one must accept it rather than pass it along with a fake humility. Being humble for humbleness's sake is only a show, a theatrics to gain from acting humble and favorable. Most people can see through fake humility and can tell whether a person is sincerely humble or not. You are better off coming across as overconfident than being faking humbleness. Humility is not about appearance nor is it only for show. Being truly humble requires integrity and deep understanding of the humanity and life in general, and it is indeed a challenge that not everyone can overcome in a lifetime.

The Foundation of Humility

True humility comes from understanding that all lives are meaningful and important. In essence, we are all the same. No one is truly greater than the other, and every life is valuable and great on its own. There is no need for discrimination once we realize that no one is different. There is no need for boasting when everyone and everything in this world are only transient and temporary. Everyone dies at one point or another, and everything owned and achieved up to that point vanishes altogether. History remembers the victors and the great, of course, but the same victors and the great are not around to bask in glory after they are all dead.

Life is short and can use some loading off of vices. While humility is certainly a virtue, it is more than just a virtue as being humble is the key and the apparatus to lift the nasty vices off your life. Pride, discrimination, condescension, greed, jealousy, and pretension can be resisted with a humble mind. Not that the resistance will always be easy and successful, but at least you are going in the right direction with a lowered head and ego. Look down not on others but on your feet and focus on moving them forward. By watching your feet and where you are going, your head will always and respectfully bow towards everyone and anyone you pass by. If you ask me, minding own business and not meddling in others' lives sounds like a humble person's attitude, all right.

9 IDLENESS

Everyone Can Use Some Break in His or Her Life

Sometimes you may feel as if you can never get enough rest. You are always tired, and fatigue makes you feel miserable. It really is a vicious cycle of negativity that puts fatigue, misery, and lethargy on a loop. The world is hectic as is, and twenty-four hours in a day is not enough time to juggle efficiently between sleep, work, and fun. The tragic part of this truth is that work is the most emphasized and enforced aspect in most our lives, more often than not, as well as more or less universal across the world and generations alike.

Taking a break, and further a proper rest at that, does not hold the same gravity as work and other celebrated virtues or ethics do when considering the vital components of life. In the competitive, fast-paced world of today, rest is regarded as a luxury that you can only afford after all things are done and achieved. Furthermore, on the same note, we feel restless and guilty even when snipping rest here and there, catching a breath for however long that is available at the moment. Meanwhile, we are reluctant to assign a specific schedule or regimen to provide for us time and effort to rest properly and, ultimately, save ourselves. Being idle, or at least allowing yourself to be idle at times, exonerates you from the guilt of resting and granting you time and space to look around and see how foolish and unhappy overworked, stringent world really is. Hopefully, by the end of this essay, you gain an insight into the merits of idleness and help yourself to achieve a better life and a better self.

Idleness vs. Laziness

Idleness is often associated and even synonymized with laziness, but that really is not the case at all. The difference between idleness and laziness is that the former is proactive while the latter is reactionary. You become lazy usually when you do not want to do something, as laziness is a form of action—or inaction—that takes up your time and energy in place of another more pressing, important task at hand. Instead, and foremost, idleness is a state of being rather than an action. Unlike laziness that occurs in response to an averse task or activity, idleness is more of an attitudinal change from specific behaviors like working and sleeping, as well as a deliberate allocation and assignment of activities in a given day and time. For example, you can be idle by both not doing anything and doing a leisurely activity while you are labeled lazy when you are either stalling or stopping from whatever on which you have been working. Admittedly, the difference is negligible overall, and the two terms are used interchangeably all the time. However, for the sake of this particular argument on the merits of idleness, allow me to elaborate on the supposed, and possibly nonexistent, difference between idleness and laziness.

The chief and thematic difference between idleness and laziness stems from the antagonistic dynamic between the two polar equals, as there exists a negatively correlated relationship in which resisting being idle from time to time wears you out and inadvertently makes you lethargic in all activities. Being idle is being smart and efficient in allocating your time and energy. Idleness is also a form of being patient and macroscopic in a way that allows you to take a step back from the action and perceive life in a slower, broader perspective. In other words, you want to be idle to prevent yourself from stooping to total laziness eventually. Some people are lazy by nature, but even people who are naturally diligent and energetic can burn themselves out to lethargic listlessness. The importance of rest is often overlooked, however, along with the acceptance of idleness as beneficial rather than detrimental in success and longevity in life.

Are the Ants Happy?

The sad reality is that many people do not know how to rest properly. The society fails to teach us many things—from that money is not a measurement of success to that happiness is absolute and not relative—and it also depreciates rest in the face of labor. Being productive is a laudatory virtue while idling is sinful, as demonstrated by the fable of "The Ant and the Grasshopper." We learn such lopsided ideals as children and, whether we remember the story vividly or not, are haunted by the subconscious voice that reminds us the fate of the idle grasshopper. The society, or rather the people who control and exploit the working population at the top, benefits from the labor and production of the people and accordingly enforces the dogma of "work first, rest second."

Perhaps you want to take a time to ask yourself whether you have been blindly chasing for dreams and roles assigned and crafted by the society while never spending enough time to reflect and find what you really want and like. Be idle for once and take the time off for yourself to ask the really important questions, to take interest in the self.

Again, the Key Is Balance

There is a certain balance in life that must be pursued and maintained to ensure a good life. Life itself is a balanced assortment of good and bad, likes and dislikes, comedies and tragedies, and so on. Work is essential for survival, and so is rest and entertainment. Life without fun and leisure is just existence, an incomplete and depressing one at that. You can only enjoy the few fun and sparse leisure when you are willing and agreeable to enjoying such perks of life. Not allowing yourself to be idle from time to time and focusing only on working—and, in turn, being productive and successful in the conventional sense at least—prevents you from being truly successful and enjoying the harmonious, fulfilled life of balance.

10 INDEPENDENCE

Stop Relying on Others, Period

Independence means more than just moving out of your parents' house. Most Americans achieve physical independence away from their increasingly nosy and patronizing parents when they enter college. From there, financial independence may take a few more years, but that arrives, too, in time. Emotional independence, however, has no set time of arrival. Thus, most people suffer from the constant need of company and comfort from others.

Physical Independence vs. Emotional Independence

Physical independence does not always guarantee emotional independence, nor is the former a prerequisite to ensure the latter. You can be emotionally independent regardless of whether you are physically alone or not. You can surround yourself with a crowd of people and still manage to be an independent, self-reliant person. Because being independent is about your will to better yourself as well as the long-term understanding of what is beneficial for you.

Depend on Yourself and Yourself Only

The only person on whom you can depend unconditionally is you. Sometimes asking for help is inevitable, but we should never exploit the good will of others. Clinging to others to fill the emotional void and physical needs in you is detrimental and toxic. Nothing is inconsequential in this world. Compassion, one of the most beautiful human emotions and deed, runs out eventually, and rather quickly when strained. No relationship can withstand an imbalanced, lopsided exchange of provisions for begging.

On the other hand, you are the most lenient and tolerant of yourself than of any other individual on earth. The relationship you have with yourself is more truthful and stronger than any other relationship you can have with another person. Take advantage of being able to depend on yourself and develop the self-reliance without fear of breaking up a relationship. Even when you hate yourself, you are stuck with yourself through the end. There is a plenty of time to develop and keep improving yourself.

Believe in Yourself

Independence stems from believing in yourself, your abilities, and your future. At some point, you have to realize that the world cannot be bend to meet your wants and needs and rather that you have to bend yourself to scrape for what you want and need. You cannot make others do your bidding or provide you for everything forever and certainly not without proper payments. The sooner you realize that self-reliance is sturdier and more lasting than any form of dependence on others, the better.

Company vs. Solitude

Company is for pleasure, not survival. Most people feel insecure and empty when they are left by themselves. They liken loneliness to sadness and boredom rather than to an opportunity to concentrate on yourself and while not disturbing others. When we congregate, we gather for reasons, be it festivities or debates. Being around others is often enjoyable and stimulating, while being alone feels stagnant and dull at times. People can prefer either situation, but the fact is that neither is essential for survival. We may thing we cannot live without the company of others, especially our loved ones, but we can—albeit sadly and reluctantly. Surely, we live to be happy and not just to stay alive. Company is good, although sometimes it can cause more problems than when left alone and make life a long, continuous headache. Moreover, relationships end, and people leave eventually. While I would never advise you to be a social pariah and shun everyone away, getting used to being alone and enjoy solitude early can only help you down the road.

11 MACROSCOPE

To Have a Macroscopic Perspective

A macroscopic mindset humbles you. We are nothing but specks of dust in a vast universe that is constantly expanding even as we speak. Even on our home planet, you are just one of seven billion people alive. While you are unique, you are not special. While you are the most important person in 'your' world, the same can be said to everyone else in 'his or her' world. Without you, your world stops, but the rest of the world live on fine, with or without you. You are the ruler and the master of your world, but even rulers and masters have their boundaries, not to mention no ruler or master lives for eternity. In the vast world we live today, there will always be someone better, richer, and smarter than you. The same can be said about the unhappier, poorer, and dumber counterparts. No matter how great or important you may be today, all you will be is a line or a paragraph on a history textbook, that is, if you are lucky to be remembered in such a way. While all of this is a welcoming news, or a bad news for the more proud people, a macroscopic perspective does more than just humble you. The most important benefit of being macroscopic is that it enables us to appreciate and make the full use of our short, limited lives.

We Are Small, and Our Problems Smaller

You are only a small part of this world, and your problems smaller. Whenever you are faced with setbacks and challenges, remind yourself that you have faced, and overcome, many difficulties before and the world did not end because of them even when it had seemed as if it would. Looking back, most problems we had in the past have remained in the past. You and the world moved on just fine, save for those occasional late-night flashbacks to your most shameful, regrettable pasts. The truth is no life will ever be free from challenges and problems. The good news is that life ends at some point, and along with it all the problems and troubles. The bad news is that we are mortals who live as if we are immortal.

The Big Picture

Think long-term while placing yourself in a bigger picture. The harsh truth is that you have at most a hundred years to live. Why waste your precious time worrying over small things, hating people who will come and go, and regretting the past that will never come back? We are given only a short time to live. Within that short span we are better off enjoying things that we love, spending time with people we love, and looking forward to the brighter tomorrow. Life is short, but it is still long enough to warrant being spent wisely and proactively. While the present is important, the future is equally, if not more, important. The past is important because it teaches you from mistakes and experience. A myopic perspective of life elongates the present and traps us into believing that future is far away and the past right at our heels. In turn, it unbalances our lives, let alone making it miserable and needlessly exigent. On the contrary, developing a far-sighted, macroscopic outlook helps maintain the balance of life and envision yourself living in the future rather than stuck in the present or trapped in the past for what feels like eternity.

The False Alarms of Life

What appears to be the matter of life and death right now is most likely a false alarm. As Nietzsche said, what does not kill you only makes you stronger, and there are only few things on world that can kill you. The costly mistakes and accidents aside, most hardships are internal and mental. Such challenges can be either ignored or overcome. While the former is an acceptable method to cope with difficulties, to ignore and pretend that a problem is solved when it really is not will make it resurface after a while. The latter method is what makes you stronger and become a better person. To overcome a challenge, however impossible it may seem, thrown in your way is a vital step towards bettering yourself. Remember that you have survived difficulties countless times before. They have all failed to kill you, and now you have become that much stronger. Take pride in the fact that you are standing today as the victor of the past.

Put on a Macroscopic Glasses

The universe is infinite while your life is finite. The macroscopic perspective contrasts your precarious, short-lived existence with the exuberant, eternal cosmos. Our lives, however, can be small or big depending on how we choose to look at them. We are indeed small beings compared to the still incomprehensible, ceaselessly growing universe. On the other hand, instead of being discouraged by and depressed over how finite and incomplete our live are, we should always try to make the full use of what we are given. We are often told to seize the day and live in the moment. Some emphasize learning from your past, while others always urge you to prepare and enjoy the future. My advice, then, is for you to follow all three suggestions. The three general teachings of temporal exploitation are not mutually exclusive in the context of a macroscopic life. You can enjoy living in the present as well as situate yourself in the negligible, humble place in history and universe while putting your past experience to good use. Only by embracing a macroscopic perspective and mind can you fully utilize the finite time in your life. We may be unimportant, fleeting specks of dust in the great universe, but that should not stop us from enjoying life and striving for greatness. In fact, nothing should discourage us from wanting to be better. After all the improvements and attempts to become a better person, I may be just another speck of dust in the space or a single-line footnote in human history. Macroscopically speaking, that does not seem like much. Then again, macroscopism is not about seeming much or doing much. It is only a perspective, a tool that should help you see things clearer and farther, like a glasses for your mind. And like a glasses, macroscopism judges nothing. It just serves your purpose, and that is that.

12 PASSION

Waking Up in the Morning, Difficult or Delightful?

You want to wake up in the morning with a sense of purpose and joy. Imagine a world where everyone welcomes the coming morning, including the universally dreaded Monday mornings. In the said world, you are always excited to start the day and finish the day as you go to sleep hoping, and knowing, a better tomorrow will follow. Despite sounding too fantastic and unrealistic, what enables such a world into a possibility is the presence of passion in one's life. A passionate person sees tomorrow as an opportunity and not another drag of existence. Passion often leads one to find and establish the meaning of life, a feat neither money nor fame alone can provide. You can be passionate about being wealthy or being famous, but all the riches in the world and the fame you can have will be meaningless without what wakes you up and keeps you going throughout your life. Money and fame come and go, but passion stays afire and afloat. Even spending money and basking in fame require certain passions related to such activities and behaviors. To have something you enjoy and want to keep doing for the rest of your life is a sign of passion moving you forward, regardless of its conspicuity or manifestation. Passion exists even when it is hidden, and it is only a matter of finding passion to complete and give meanings to life.

Searching for Passions

Many people do not know how to find their passions, let alone know that they have them in the first place. The first objective, then, is to have faith that somewhere out there and deep in your heart, a passion exists. You may not know it yet and have not found it until now, but it is better to be late than never. After having established that you indeed possess a passion and are willing to explore it to existence, you must consciously put in an effort to know yourself. Through reflection as well as trial-and-errors, you start figuring out what you like, what fulfills your life, what you do well, and what you can continue doing for the rest of your life. You want to envision yourself performing the passion of your life as you take your last breath. You want to find the passion that takes your breath away every second of your life. For example, most writers wish they would die with a pen in their hand, mid-sentence. Dancers would never leave the stage as long as they can even barely stand, and singers would sing themselves to the eternal sleep, to literally the last breath passing though their lungs. The prospect of dying with ongoing passion denotes a life spent in full and that a single lifetime alone is not enough to fulfill the thirst and drive to enjoy and utilize the limited days we are given.

Existence + Meaning = Life

Passion distinguishes a life from a mere existence, for it elevates 'just' living to a just living. Without passion, you are prone repeat daily lives mechanically just to put the food on the table, a state of being that is the perfect example of a purposeless life. Wishing to never wake up next morning or to count days toward your death are pathetic symptoms of lives that see neither hope nor fun within. The difference between depression and 'de-passion' is that the patients ailing from the former condition cannot stand life due to both the psychological and physiological problems while the group suffering from the latter predicament are too lazy and listless to even put end to their pitiful existences.

Direction, Control, and Future

Life is an arbitrary, unpredictable journey even at its finest, but passion makes it unique as passion gives you the identity of who you are. You can call whatever your life is by what you want. It is your life, after all. You can will it to become anything, make your own future, change everything around you to your own liking. Without passion, however, none of this is possible. You lack the central character inside you that can dictate such decisions with dominion and direction. The character that you wish to become and are capable of doing so simply cannot present him or herself before you when the dispassionate outlook of life conforms to the bare minimal requirements of survival and social acceptance. You have to be great, want to be great, and let your life flower instead of sinking low and crawl with the rest of the faceless, spineless nobodies of the mass.

The Next Human Evolution

Passion is not only a purpose of life but is a parent of more purposes. Life is comprised of countless choices and the chain reactions among those same choices. Passion guides you to make the right, if not any, choice as passion combines your past, present, and future needs, desires, and ambitions into one cohesive and comprehensive core of character that is you. With each passionate pace you walk into more paths of problems and possibilities. The good news is that no road ahead is the wrong walk to take as long as passion, the sum of your belief, hope, and confidence, guides you all the way. Yesterday you wrote a song, and today you get to sing. Today you write a poem, and tomorrow you throw away the garbage it is and write another one. Tomorrow I will write another essay, next week I will have written enough to publish a book.

You look forward to what will come before you. Just this morning I sprang from my bed eager to type away on my laptop. For ten years my fingers have danced atop the keyboard, and my mind has been on a marathon next to dashing words and jumpy insight. My passion of writing has not only kept in the race me all those years but made me who I am today.

Passion is truly a magic, the last one left for the mankind as well as the one to push it to the next level.

13 PATIENCE

Time Is Mighty

It was not the curiosity that killed the cat, but rather the impulsiveness that followed. Curiosity has always helped the mankind. The inquisitive attitude towards nature and life has led to many ground-breaking discoveries and inventions such as gravity—in attempt to explain for apples falling to the ground—and spacecrafts used for landing on the moon— simply because people had long wanted to see what it was like up there. Curiosity is good, as is the proper and thorough preparation being put up to quell a given curiosity. Likewise, every sensation and excitement in this world is beneficial as long as it is not rushed and forced. Even the most deadly sins can be justified with proper outlets and executions. Lust, for example, can lead to either violent sexual crimes or fiery romantic courtships. Envy, instead of feeling deprived and resentful, can motivate one to equal himself or herself to the envious target. The difference of each outcome lies in one chief attitude and mindset: patience. Patience enables you to look farther ahead and gives you time to prepare accordingly. More importantly, with patience—and in time— things get done.

Patience Lost Today

Today's world has become more fast-paced than ever thanks to technological developments and the concomitant improved living standards that accommodate all the luxuries and perks of industrial and domestic advancements, and we are accustomed to getting instant results and feedback. While such a swiftness is convenient and generally helpful in most aspects of our lives, there are some drawbacks to living in an instantaneous, techno-driven society. For example, with the advent and prevalence of electronic mails, we can no longer experience the bittersweet sentiment of waiting for a reply that normally took days and even weeks to come by. We can still write handwritten letters and exchange them via land mail, but that nostalgic touch is forever lost for us, all the more if we try to force and replicate the past. Cellular phones have imprisoned us rather than freed us with the constant calls and the sense of being chained to our contacts anytime and anywhere, at home or outside, at rest or at work, asleep or awake. The fact that everyone can be reached anytime with only seconds of delay through a mobile phone has only made our lives more hectic, tense, and nerve-racking. Internet has made everything easier, faster, and more accessible, including crimes and felonies happening ubiquitously, anonymously, and globally. This is not a lament on the loss of slower life and times. Change is inevitable whether it is for the good or the bad. The sad part, however, is that a fast-paced life is prone to rushed results and careless consequences when it really does not have to be that way.

Life Is Short, but Not Short Enough

Life is short, but it is long enough for you to make thousands of happy memories, or bad memories if you are not careful. Time is fluid, fair, and relative. You cannot stop time just as you can not stop water flowing from mountaintop to a sea. Time is given to everyone from the birth, free of charge, although the duration and when it all ends varies from person to person. How you use your time is totally up to you. Time is , indeed, not entirely independent of wealth and health, as being rich and being healthy can drastically change how one spends his or her time. But in the end, however relatively time has been spent and differed, everyone runs out of time and dies. Whether such a fact comforts you or not, that is the truth: time is fluidly fleeing, fairly fatal, and relatively irrelevant. We can never beat Father Time. The only way to approach and confront time is to be patient and let it pass. Good things happen as well as bad things, and we try our best to let only good things happen to us and stop bad things from happening. Again, we can only try because life gives us a mixed set of fortunes and miseries alternating randomly. We try and remember that 'this too will pass away,' however good or bad 'this' is.

Practicing Patience

Look far ahead and remain calm. Be prepared for anything that future will throw away at you in order to protect yourself, and maintain calmness to fool yourself into believing that everything is, and will be, fine. Understandably, such an attitude is easier said than to be actually done. Patience is a trait that can only be learned and understood rather than with which one is born. An infant or a toddler knows no patience in want of food, toys, and love. Children are impatient because they have lived for only a short time and should be excused for—and gradually taught against—such impatient behaviors. Adults do not get the same pass as children, naturally, and yet the world is full of childish, immature people who just demand and desire without check. More often than not, the childishness and immaturity of the said people are the causes of their unhappiness, as well as that of those around them. Impatience in a person is as unappealing as it is tiresome. Impatient people are never contented at the moment and always rush to the end, leading to incomplete and unstable results not too unlike their own lives. On the contrary, the most saintly and sagacious figures in history all displayed patience as one of their virtues. Jesus patiently waited for the right timing to prove people wrong and teach them time after time; he even waited for three full days to come out of the grave to let everyone know that he did not fake death for a short time but rather that he was raised from the dead. Buddha, too, meditated under a Bodhi Tree for seven weeks without moving to gain enlightenment. Confucius lived his entire life an unemployed scholar who waited for the right prince to listen to his advice and teachings and died without the acknowledgement and respect he is getting now thousands of years after his lifetime. Of course, not everyone is or can be like Jesus, Buddha, or Confucius. At the very least, however, we should take after their examples and practice even a momentary patience in our lives, not because we want to be famous or want to be remembered posthumously, but because how fulfilling and meaningful the lives of the said saints turned out to be in the end. Your life, I dare say, is a fraction of the lives of Jesus, Buddha, and Confucius in terms of turbulence and hardships. Accordingly, just with a fraction of their patience and endurance—namely three hours until forgiveness, seven days to look back on your life, and a year-long search for your true vocation and passion—you will be more than fine with your life.

14 PHILOSOPHY

Philosophy as a Tool

Do not let the word 'philosophy' scare you, or
bore you either. The study of philosophy is,
indeed, tedious and boring. Philosophies also
feel irrelevant and detached due to their
ancient and archaic origins and despite how
timeless such great philosophies claim to be.
You may ask why you should bother caring
what the so-called philosophers of hundreds
and even thousands of years ago thought and
wrote down. Surely, you do not want to
complicate things even further by bringing in
something as esoteric and extraneous as
philosophy into your life. Yet the truth is
philosophy does not have to be complicated at
all. Philosophy as an academic field may be a
headache, but we do not have to, or want to,

study it. Practical philosophy, or philosophy as a tool, is the one for which we should all aim. Moreover, it is an adoption of a system and learning to think systematically and logically within our understanding of life and the world around us that should be practiced more often and thoroughly amongst us.

Daily Philosophies

Everyone has a philosophy, just that it is not as celebrated or brilliant as the more famous ones. More often than not, many people do not realize that they even possess a philosophy of their own. The way you cut your toast in half is a simple act with accumulated philosophies and preferences of all your experience with eating toasts. Cutting it diagonally may fit more securely in your large hand or you simply like your toast in a triangular shape. Cutting off the crust may agree more with your foul, spiky tongue who is silently yet sharply protesting in your place about going to that dreadful place called 'work.' To put it philosophically, your relationship with toasts and morning rituals may be summarized as, "A triangular toast to a spectacular start," or "No crust in your mouth, no roust for the day." Silly examples aside, many of life's littlest things are made up of your preferences and prudences. Your decision to wake up early every morning to avoid stressful traffic is the result of your learned behavior of and success after compromising sleep hours on bed for the later comfort at the car. Your abstinence of alcohol during weeknights is your sense of responsibility and being cautious of having a nightmare of a time at work the next day. Philosophy is not always and necessarily present in a lengthy, thick published hardcover book. It is present everywhere in your life, even without you noticing it.

Philosophy as an Operating System

Philosophy is like an operating system with which you run your life. Just as it does not matter whether a computer runs on a Windows, Macintosh, or Linux, you do not need to be a proclaimed philosopher of one branch to lead a good life. Nor do you have to own or endorse a fancy, famous philosophy to stay alive—just as many people use the computers and the smarthpones freely and conveniently so long as they can open web browsers and type on word processors. The operating system analogy is not a knock on the fellow simple, technophobes but rather an encouragement and a welcome sign for everyone in that one does not have to be professional and knowledgeable about something to exploit and benefit from it. There are people who—like me—believe that a computer is as good as the keyboards click in a right, tap-dancy way and the word processor can open up twenty documents at the same time. This is actually a great, simple philosophy for a writer to have. Likewise, if one were to say, "If people never did silly things, nothing intelligent would ever get done," without knowing or even caring about who Wittgenstein is and proceeded to go out of his or her way to do the stupidest thing imaginable for the hopefully concomitant intelligent under-standing, then so be it. There is nothing—and no one—to judge, really.

The Shoulders of the Giants

Your problems have already been had and solved by someone else in the past. While not identical in every aspect, lives are more or less similar to one another with shared problems and universal joys alike. What this means is that the smarter, wiser people of the past have already provided answers to the most frequently occurring human problems and questions in books and teachings. From conquering happiness to pondering about life's meanings, every critical epiphany is available to those willing to search for it.

Take It Easy

I am not asking you to invent a new philosophy. You do not come up with a new philosophy, but rather tailor the existing ones to fit your needs. You also do not have to indoctrinate it to existence as just being aware that your life has a systematic philosophy working and supporting you is sufficient to get you going.

System and Consistency

Being philosophical implies being systematically thoughtful and consistent based on your beliefs, standards, and integrity. What being philosophical does not mean is that you sound pompously knowledgeable and refer to Socrates or Hegel in every other sentence.

Thinking systematically and consistently is the key to being philosophical. The foundation of the system of all your thoughts cannot be borrowed from else where. That part has to be crafted by you. Even just to assemble your ideas into a coherent system requires time, experience, reflection, and, most importantly, determination. The time will come when you feel as if you need to get a hold of your life, to structure and organize your life in a way that suits your needs, wants, and tendencies.

Experience will be your materials as well as the cost to build such a structure. Reflection and consideration will force you to think inward as well as out of the box to change yourself as well as fit yourself into the mold of a system that is the most ideal and optimal. Throughout this process, you need to will yourself to become the person you want to become, to become the better and even the best you can be with the new functioning, stable system of thoughts, conducts, and outlooks regarding and of life. To me, at least, that is what being philosophical and having a philosophy as a core system in life means. In a way, it is a philosophy of its own, albeit unprincipled and hardly research-worthy. I am neither Kant nor Sartre and will never catch up to the ranks of them (nor, mind you, do I plan to), but what I want to point out of all this is that if I can come up with and flaunt a faulty philosophy like this, then so can you.

15 PROACTIVITY

Look Ahead and Forward

Your past affects your present, and your present your future. Yet many people seem to disregard this simple common sense, not out of ignorance but rather out of fatigue and even laziness. Most depressed and lethargic people have relinquished taking control of their lives and let life sway them in any flow it turns and takes. "Whatever will be, will be," sounds sweet and sagacious in that one classic song, but there is a better alternative than to throw the towel and parrot that "future is not ours to see." For your information, the adage "que sera sera" makes more sense combined with another old saying, "God helps those who help themselves." After putting in all the efforts and work you can, the rest is up to fate and the heavens to decide, whether to reward you or judge for your worth and dedication. In that case, whatever will be, indeed, will be.

On the contrary to facing the future with a sense of purpose, sometimes we place more emphasis on the past than necessary. The past is nothing more than a source of reflection and awareness for you to utilize living on the present and into the future. Clinging onto and regretting over past events feel like a second nature to many of us while they provide more hindrance than benefits. The direction towards which you should look is forwards, not backwards. The sad reality, however, is that far too many of us dread facing the next day, especially the Mondays after weekends and holidays.

Future Is Everything

The past is gone, while the future still awaits. The past has already served its role in making who you are today, but the future is where you can become the best you can be. Tomorrow, admittedly, is not always joyous and full of promises. Work and other stressful stimuli seem to be abundant and even prevalent compared to the few and scarce reasons to be happy and hopeful. Nonetheless, to apprehend coming days of stress and pressure or to look for happy, joyous tomorrows is just a matter of forcing yourself to take which attitude. Blind optimism is just as dangerous than outright pessimism, but there is no choice but to be blindly optimistic towards the future that we can never foresee and predict one-hundred-percent in any given time. Besides, you are not being naively optimistic when it comes to hoping for a better tomorrow. For a starter, you must work hard to make the happy future you dream to be a reality. Furthermore, sometimes willing for good, happy days to come is enough to recognize and perceive any day to be a good day. Call it a cognitive bias if you want, but you can find joy and pleasure in any smallest reason and event as long as you are willing to embrace it as such. The same can be said for finding despair in even the most comforting reasons, sadly and more frequently among today's people as it seems.

Take Control of Life Rather Than Let Life Control You

Never let life take control away from you. The most important part of being proactive is taking control of your life. You are in control of what you say, what you do, whom you meet, where you go, and when you do all of these things. The "why's" of all of your life activities are trickier, but for the sake of this essay series, let us deem them "to become a better person." In this particular discussion, why you act, say, meet others, and go where you want or have to go is to have a better tomorrow, a better future. To have a sense of purpose, ultimate or subsidiary, helps you keep a firm grip on the rein over your life. Not having a purpose of your life often leads to chaotic, disoriented course of life that this very essay seeks to correct.

When you feel as if you have lost control over your lives, or when all hopes seem to have been lost, just remember that you can gain the control back anytime you put your mind to the task and that hopes are lost and found all the time, interchangeably and inevitably. Feeling as if you have lost control at work, slaving away for your boss and company? Quitting from such a toxic environment will be for the best, but if that is simply not possible, at least you have your paychecks and off-work hours to which you can look forward. One day you hope you want to marry, and a few months into marriage you now hope for some miraculous, safe way to get a divorce.

The truth is life is never perfect, nor are you. Life is chaotic and uncontrollable in its given state. The merit lies in that we still have to try to perfect and control life the best we can as possible. When to imperfect beings collide, namely life and a human being, disasters are bound to happen. And amidst those catastrophes are flashes and cracks of bliss and hope that we just have to snatch and preserve with a strong will and a clenched fist. Life is a war, and you just have to fight back, and with strategies.

The Best Way to Predict a Future

The best way to predict a future is to create one. Actively, and proactively, build your own future so you know what it will look like. Make your present the blueprint to realizing your dream. Being prudent and far-sighted in making every action and decision is the key to becoming proactive. That is your strategy against winning the war against life. Life is the battlefield and the enemy. Life is just a big cluster of opponents and challenges, and sometimes you are mixed up in that party as well. Therefore, when you are being proactive and taking control of your life, you have to watch out for yourself as well. Your mistakes, laziness, and occasional despairs are yours and your worst enemies. You can never slay them for good but rather keep them on watch and in constant scuffles. Win or lose, the process never stops, and in between those victories and losses you become only better as a person, so long as you do not give up and keep the fight going. You are a victor just for hanging in there.

16 PROFESSIONALISM

Passion vs. Professionalism

Simply put, to be professional is to be proud of and be responsible for what you do for living. Being good at your job is always a plus, but professionalism means more than just competence. You can be bad at your job—for now at least—but professionalism can help you keep pushing yourself until you become better and great one day. A penniless musician will never give up music even if it means he will have to live on the streets. A rookie athlete may be the worst player in the league but not for long. Professionalism fuels people and helps them keep doing what they do.

The same can be said about passion, however, specifically in regards to passion's role in perseverance and optimism, but professionalism is quite different form passion in that the former is an attitude while the latter is an emotion. In fact, professionalism is passion without the fiery, subjective attitude. We hear people say, "Be professional" about something from time to time. The phrase denotes detaching one's self from the situation and solve the problem objectively and efficiently. In fact, "Be professional" is the exact opposite of "Be passionate." The contrast attests to how you can be professional without being passion-ate about your work.

You Matter

Your profession impacts the world. No matter who says otherwise, you are a valuable asset to the society. It is important for you to have faith in yourself and pride over the fact that you are a responsible human being who is capable of and diligent at putting food on the table through your hard work and labor. Making a living is a huge feat that is disregarded and taken for granted by many. We forget too easily that we are battling for our lives day in and night out. Perhaps we are too tired and fed up with existence to take the small victories and prizes when and where we can. Such is a situation that leads to a life without meaning and purpose.

Enter professionalism, and possibly to the rescue. Being professional means you are past the point where you doubt and question yourself. You are assured that you are not a nobody. You are a professional, and that means exactly that. Professionalism may not make your life more fun and exciting, but it will give you a sense of direction and deliberation. You are working as professional at your field, and that establishes a fact that you play a role, small or big, in our society.

To Love the Unlovable

Not too many people love their jobs, quite understandably. Work is rarely fun and comfortable; most jobs out in the world are repetitive, stressful, and boring rather than refreshing, exciting, and relaxing. Even the most exciting and the so-called 'dream job's become dull and sickening with time and wear. Work is generally hated and loathed because we work to earn money. Money is a limited commodity that is scarce and hoarded by a few select percentage of the population, let alone nonexistent and imaginary in certain markets and banks. We need money to survive, at least in a civilized society, and there are way too many people occupying the crowded civilized lands of today's world. What all of this implies is that work is stressful and unpleasant by design. Work is an war of acquirement as well as competition, and the stake of each battle is none other than our own lives. No wonder people would rather forget about the meaning of life and instead live on blindly and dumbly. The world is a stressful environment, and we are forced to work under it, for it, and amongst it.

Enter professionalism, this time definitely for the rescue. We need a purpose, and professionalism grants us just that. We are not just working, but we are working as professionals. That alone means something amidst the global war and battle going on about and around money, both physical and phantasmal. We all need a meaning to go on with our lives. When you are being professional, you are efficient and to the point. Extend and expand that professional attitude towards life. Embrace it, and take control.

No Way Around to It: Work Is Work

Professionalism, in a nutshell, is just another word for 'commitment.' Whether you love your job or not, you do your best with what you are given and to whom you owe your service. To proclaim love for something that you truly do not love is a torture in itself. On the other hand, professionalism requires not your love but rather your sense of responsibility and compromise. You do not have to love what you do for living, but the least you can do is not making it another reason to hate your existence.

Work is work. Sometimes you feel like you would rather die than go to work and labor yourself all day only to come home and repeat the same process day after day. The prospect of retirement and even the transient weekends that seem to evaporate as soon as they arrive are the only things you look forward to and keep yourself alive. Perhaps you have tried to instill passion into your work at one point. You tried your best to like everything and anything about your work at first but to no avail. Most people are like that: miserably working and hating every minute of their work life. The truth is that passion requires luck and sacrifices. Luck is something you cannot control, but sacrifices you can. In short, in order for passion to be present in your life, you have to compromise and concentrate your resources, namely time, pleasures, and comforts. A hungry painter would rather starve to death than to give up paining, resorting to drawing anything, or even working at McDonald's for years to come, to draw what he or she really wants to draw. Passion is often like an affliction, and most people in this world are rarely susceptible to such a syndrome. Whether that is good news or bad news, you can be the judge, but as for how to live your life and determine whether work is work or work means life, you have to more than just judge. Most people are contented to be just professional and not really passionate about their jobs, and such a compromise is perfectly fine and laudable as is. The worst possible case is, of course, when you are neither professional nor passionate.

17 READINESS

Bad Things Happen

You become a better person by being mentally prepared for both the best and the worst possible cases. What this means, sadly, is that you have to be constantly on your toes, not letting anything take you by surprise. You have to be constantly reminded that anything can happen and that you have no choice but to accept whatever the outcome and move as long as you live. Admittedly, this is a lifelong challenge that is easier said than done.

No one can predict future, and unexpected surprises happen all the time. Why not just relax and let life take over, one may ask. Besides, surprises are not always bad. There are good surprises, such as windfall luck and fortunes from winning the lottery or inheriting wealth from a distant relative's obscure will. But those come very rarely, and we are much better off expecting only bad surprises in life. Therefore, expect and ready yourself against all bad possibilities and outcomes because not only are they more common than their counterpart lucks and fortunes but also because you always benefit from preparing yourself against the worst odds and scenarios imaginable.

The Worst Possible Case

Being far-sighted is the key to being ready at all times. You can embrace any future event if you have already foreseen it in your mind. The best clairvoyance you can fool yourself to possess is to always imagine the worst possible scenario. By having simulated the worst possible case in your head, you are able to deal with any situation and even take comfort when the worst scenario does not happen. My suggestion for you is to be optimistic with what you have and have had, but be pessimistic for what will and may happen. Lower your expectations to better ready yourself against hardships and misfortunes in the future. You may hope that tomorrow is better than today, but do not bet on it to happen. Tomorrow may as well be the worst day of your life, and you will have to live and fight through it nonetheless. Even when tomorrow comes and is not as bad as you have feared it to be, you will still be glad to have kept your guard up and protected yourself from naive hopefulness and unwarranted optimism.

Studying from the Past

Anticipation comes from experience, meaning you simply cannot forget and let go of your past easily. We are often told to forget bad past and move on towards brighter future. Yet we do not exist without our past, and while the future comes to you without your say in which manner, you are in full control of your past in terms of how you view it and utilize it to your advantage. You control what you can control, and the past is right there for you as long as you do not willfully forget or obsessively regret. History repeats itself, and you as an individual has a set of fixed and redundant tendencies that recur throughout your life. While many events are caused outside of our influence, the most direct and intimate events occur because of our actions, words, and behaviors. By knowing yourself fully and being careful not to repeat the same mistakes may prevent unwanted consequences to hurt you in the future. Clinging onto the past is not always unhealthy when you hold onto it proactively. The past is there for you as a material for teaching and warning yourself in the future and never as a point in time for retreating from the present and regret regressively.

Ready and Reliable

Readiness grants you calmness and composure. We all want to be calm and in control even in the most difficult times. Someone who is unperturbed and composed all the time makes others feel comfortable and calm as well. People depend on such a person and deem him or her reliable and trustworthy. While that alone is a great social perk to have, we do not want to acquire and master constant readiness just for others to like us. The person that benefits the most from readiness is none other than the self. It is for the quality of your life that you should try to become a ready, poised person.

Control What Is Controllable

We can never control our future, but at least we can decide how we can react. To help reacting more calmly, we should train ourselves to be ready for anything that comes in our way. Simulating all kinds of possible outcomes certainly helps, and if you had to choose one scenario out of all, you should always imagine the worst possible case to prepare your mind so that any surprise from good to bad can be embraced in a rather relieved, readied manner.

To be constantly ready is a difficult task that requires a serious series of practice and a definite sense of purpose. You practice being ready through mental simulation and getting used to the unpredictable and seemingly cruel courses of life. To be ready for anything and everything is a sign of maturity and sagacity often, but not always, observed in the more aged population that has seen and experienced more than the younger generations. This does not mean that readiness and calmness come only through age and experience. The most important criterion for readiness is the attitude, the awareness of its vital role in helping you live through your life. The purpose of being ready against all and in all times is to build you strong and adept in this lifelong voyage that will have to go through high tides and stormy weathers. A ship sails while expecting to be hit by waves and typhoons on its journey. Life is not always sunny and beautiful, nor should you hope for it to be always so. Challenges and difficulties are parts of life, and as powerless and only able to control so many aspects of life, we tighten our grips and brace ourselves against the coming storm, and the next, never prevailing but at least fighting and ready to take on the worst enemy, and so on.

18 REFLECTION

The Only Way to Really Grow Up

To reflect on the self is the only way to mature
and really learn from experience. Yet not too
many people practice self-reflection daily, or
even at all. Through reflection, you review your
past actions and thoughts, followed by making
corrections and adjustments accordingly. In
other words, reflection is the de facto process
of improving yourself. This entire essay series
is meaningless without this particular entry of
emphasizing the importance of understanding
and practicing reflection to better the self.
There is simply no other way around it.
Without reflection, there is no foundation of
growth.

Aging vs. Maturing

Many people just age without maturing. They simply grow old without ever really becoming better today than yesterday. Thus the popular saying that 'People do not change easily.' The change is all the more difficult in the positive direction. People generally stay the same unless circumstances call for them to change, but adults, unlike children, are rarely challenged and forced to change themselves. As a result, life becomes boring and uniform and most of us are stuck with the same problems and routines of life at forty as we were at thirty. Life, however, does not have to be that way all the time. The reason for a stagnant, immutable life is the lack of reflection. The absence of reflection affects people in a way that they lose the opportunity look back on themselves and figure out what went wrong and what could have been better. Understandably, life is just too hectic and hassling for one to patiently and consistently learn from mistakes and correct the past. Only when we consciously try to make time and effort to reflect on the past mistakes and wrongs can we prevail against the biggest enemies in our lives, namely ourselves.

Simply Experiencing vs. Learning from Experiences

Experiencing and learning from experiences are two different matters. The former just happens with or without one's consent or control over it. The latter, on the other hand, is a deliberate action taken with a purpose to make the self and the life better and rid of mistakes and faults. Reflection is just another word for learning from the past experiences. We experience all sorts of things as we live on naturally. To take an extra effort to look back and review our daily and natural experiences is equivalent to living your life again. As we re-live the crucial and critical moments of our past, we teach ourselves whether to avoid such moments at all cost or do our best to recreate as many similar moments and occasions as possible. Reflection applies to both good and bad experiences. History repeats itself, and our past is the blueprint to our future. By constantly reviewing our past and making optimal corrections about ourselves, we are better prepared for the future that we want and can build on proactively.

The Past: Enemy or Ally?

The past can be your enemy as well as your ally. The same can be said about ourselves. More often than not, life is about battling the self and performing better against the us of yesterdays. The world is full of enemies without adding ourselves to the unpleasant pool. Whether we spend the rest of our lives fighting against ourselves or along with ourselves is totally up to you. Reflection requires us to confront ourselves, both of the present and the past. Many people simply take our consciousness and conscientiousness for granted, that our natural tendencies and proclivities cannot be helped nor corrected in the face of bigger, more direct emergencies and exigencies. The truth is that all important changes come from within the self. The embarrassing pasts that you choose to conveniently ignore and forget for the time being will inevitably come back to haunt you and face you as an enemy in the future. Before that happens, we have to tame and master our faulty selves and mistakes we have been and made in the past. The past can be your textbook for learning and a sandbox for creating the better future. It can also be your worst nightmare, both literally in your sleep and eventually in your future, if you naively believe that mistakes happen only once and a fault can resurface unless managed and corrected in the first place.

You Shall Not Forget Just Because

To forget is to make you vulnerable. You are your worst enemy when you let past mistakes repeat over and over while learning nothing from the disasters and embarrassments that you carelessly and foolishly believe will not happen again. While forgetting some unfortunate, uncontrollable events in the past is a must, we should not let every past be wasted and forgotten in such a way. Only the freak accidents and chance events that are beyond our control of prevention and expectation deserve to be forgotten, while the rest have to be remembered and reviewed for future references. It is better to remember everything than to forget everything, at least in terms of preparing yourself for the future. To remember everything is, of course, a stressful attempt and a near-impossible task. Between remembering and forgetting, the difference is the temporal status of the pain and the stress, whether to be stressed now for remembering or in the future by forgetting. Sadly, reflection requires you to remember, and the concomitant pain associated with reliving and reviving every past is unavoidable. Yet to be in pain now consciously and willingly is better to be in pain later unexpectedly and vulnerably. The con-sequence of forgetting for the sake of the present comfort is to be struck by misfortunes and disasters that could have been prevented with foresight and remembrance. Life can go either way based on which type of pain you prefer. It is up to you to choose between an enduring, conscious pain that you inflict on yourself to become a better, more prepared and stable person and a foolish, perennial pain that recurs time after time that everyone but yourself knows could have been avoided and is caused by none other than yourself. In the case of the latter, you let your reputation take a hit as well and yourself remembered as a careless, nearsighted person who is prone to problems and hopeless of improving at all. No one likes such a notoriety, let alone be around a person with one.

19 RETICENCE

Talking vs. Listening

Speech is silver, silence is golden. This timeless adage is known to many but practiced by a few, let alone appreciated. The world recognizes good talkers and may even celebrate them— namely the lawyers and the television show hosts—while the patient listeners and silent sages are, naturally, unnoticed and taken for granted. All of us, however, are both talkers and listeners in our lives. There is nothing harmful in listening. Listening to lectures, for example, is still the collegiate standard of learning. You can learn, think, and reflect while listening. Talking, on the other hand, is the bearer and propagator of problems. We have all experienced those embarrassing and dooming occasions where our tongues decided to act independently against our brains. In a heated talk or meaningless rambling, we often say things that we have never meant to say out loud, let alone known that such thoughts existed in us. Call them revelations or Freudian slips, those mistakes could have been prevented with a shut mouth for all things considered.

Exposing Yourself to Dangers

To say is to expose, and to expose is to endanger. We all know and have experienced how liberating it feels to talk out your mind and express your feelings without restraint. Well, that particular liberation comes at a cost just as everything else that is good in life comes with an inevitable price tag. Life is only fair in that you can never have too much good stuff going on without any consequence. Party too much, you suffer the next day. Smoke too much, hello cancer and other nasty cardio-respiratory diseases. Love too much, no matter how perfect a relationship, the love is not returned the same way. But most of us know for which we are bargaining. In return for some temporary peace of mind and letting off steam by talking away our problems, we let the listener, and the world, know that such problems exist and that we are vulnerable to them. The moment we talk our problems and weaknesses to existence, they never go away. They come to haunt us back in one way or another, sooner or later. For example, that evil boss you have been complaining about to your trusted coworker? First off, there is no such thing as trustworthy, reliable colleague or coworker. They are just like you, miserable and reluctant individuals in the workplace forever regretting having entered it in the first place. Words get out eventually and the evil boss may know of your sentiments against him or her. That seems fine, since the hate is mutual, but the worst outcome of a little gossip is that the people around you now know for who you are: a whiner and a complainer. Even if you are otherwise perfect, that one complaint will cost you your established status. If such a scenario does not bother you, then imagine confiding your secrets to your lover or a partner. The result is the same: you become vulnerable as you are exposed. Besides, no one likes or cares about others' problems. To listen to whining requires either unconditional love or ulterior motive such as a future plan to exploit the divulged information for personal gains.

If you think I am exaggerating and that one gossip or complaint cannot be all that bad, remember that life is an accumulation of experience and feelings. A fallen reputation is hard to be raised up again, just as an instance of disappointment and condescension is hard to erase from memory. Keep it to yourself when it comes to expressing what is troubling you if you can in order to avoid it boomerang it back at you in the future by someone you trusted or from a totally unexpected direction. Being secretive is not as evil when it comes to protecting a relationship from falling. Honesty is a virtue, but too much honesty is like a fire that burns everything, including the one you have been trying to protect and keep it warm. Never be blindly honest where you have to watch who, what, and why you are being honest towards. Being honest does not mean you can do whatever you want in the name of honesty. By doing whatever you want, such as talking excessively and mindlessly, you are bound to destroy and hurt in the process.

You Need Two to Talk

The best way to prevent yourself from talking too much is to isolate yourself. There are other methods too, but being alone is the best and the surest way to execute out of them all. You simply cannot expose yourself and babble like a fool if you have no one with whom to talk. Isolating yourself to total solitude also means getting rid of any connection to anyone else, meaning no phone call or messenger application is allowed. Solitude may be the best way to ensure forced reticence on your part, but it is, admittedly, not easy to isolate yourself completely in today's world of accessibility and connection. Besides, denying yourself from the perks and benefits of the society and socialization through isolation may feel as if the effort is counterintuitive and counterproductive. You cannot be truly or forever alone in today's world. My suggestion, then, is to opt in for selective solitude, a practice of isolating yourself from people for specific purposes only. Just for once, when you feel like you are going to explode and barrage on someone excessively and meaninglessly for hours, think through how that will come back to you in the future, how you will debase your image as a collected person by emotionally harassing the listener.

You are, of course, welcome to talk away your worries and thought as you have been doing your entire conscious life and continue to do so for the rest of it. I am just giving you an alternative that can maybe change your life.

A Means of Protecting Yourself

Reticence requires practice as well as determination and awareness. As you grow older, you realize that people are not as innocent and understanding as you used to know them when you were younger. With age people become wiser, but not necessarily kinder. Especially in today's competitive, individualistic society, many of us are not afraid to exploit others for our own good. The world is a harsh place filled with more enemies than allies to your side. The sooner you realize this, again, the better off you are.

20 SELF-AWARENESS

Know Thyself

'Know thyself.' Thanks to this fabricated prophecy originally intended for confusion, Socrates became only wiser, if not the wisest man in the human history. The ancient adage that urges people to know and question themselves has survived time and tested, and stymied, millions for the past two millennia. The longevity and the potency of those two simple words, in turn, attest to how difficult it is to succeed in really knowing one's self. Objectivity against the self is quite a challenge to achieve, not to mention dangerous at times as objectivity may be confused with needless negativity and unnecessary strictness. In spite of such difficulties, we have to truly know ourselves to even begin improve ourselves and become better people, not to mention be able to recognize our better selves when such a time comes.

Nobody Is Perfect

No one is perfect, and everyone has problems of his or her own. What most people fail to recognize is that most problems are caused by themselves and not by some uncontrollable outside forces. For example, the problem of being surrounded by hostile people can be solved chiefly and effectively by removing yourself from the vicinity of the said people. The problem is multifaceted in that even though the hostility of people itself is indeed problematic, the bigger, and remaining, problem is that no measure is taken to distance yourself and end the ongoing torment. In such a case, the inactivity of making changes on your part are the cause of prolonging and extenuating the problem. Furthermore, the dislike itself may have been caused entirely by you while you, like most people, fail to recognize and admit that you are at fault foremost and in the first place.

Self-awareness in the conventional sense is often regarded negatively, as demonstrated by the generic example above, while it is not entirely so when taken into a broader, constructive context. Being self-aware indubitably denotes highlighting your faults and complexes. If it just ends there, then self-awareness is indeed negative, detrimental, and averse to improving the self. But self-awareness does more than just uncovering your problems as it helps you solve those problems going forward. Self-awareness is a two-step process of recognizing problems followed by implementing changes and solution. Recognizing a problem is the first step to solving it. You cannot find problems unless you look for them first, especially if those are problems are innate and within you. You can only improve yourself through and after solving your problems.

Objectifying Yourself

We should pay more attention to ourselves regardless of whether self-awareness leads to self-love or self-loathing. In fact, self-love and self-awareness should be independently adapted. Self-love is embracing everything— good or bad—about you while self-awareness is more objective and evaluative. What self-awareness does is that it recognizes and then possibly diagnoses any problem you have.

Self-love is not enough. You have to back it up with the objective, diagnostic approach of being self-aware and willing to solve any problem you have.

The Universe That Is You

You are a universe of your own. You are worth a deep look, and you warrant a profound and comprehensive understanding. The only person who can do such things is you yourself. Only you can do that.

While your days are limited, the number of possibilities for you out there is infinite.

21 SELF-CONTROL

The Purpose of Self-Control

Self-control is a manifestation of responsibility, maturity, and intelligence combined. Through self-control you protect and sustain the life for which you are, and should absolutely be, responsible. Only the truly mature and experienced understand the importance of self-control, while the fools and the ignorant disregard self-control altogether and end up destroying their lives through either excessive indulgence or unchecked greed. The purpose of self-control is not, of course, to show others how responsible, mature, and sagacious you are. Self-control improves your life and is for your benefits only, although the world populated with more prudent people will indubitably benefit the entire humankind.

The Middle Path

Excess kills you just as surely and unpleasantly as deficiency does. Hunger and gluttony are both lethal in extended, extreme cases. Thirst and drowning are another pair of polar opposites that yield the same consequence. Hypothetical and metaphysical discussions aside, it is evident that moderation is the optimal practice for survival. Moderation, in essence, is an effort to maintain balance between your desires and necessities. Self-control does not have to be total abstinence in most cases as moderation works better in some cases. In fact, indulging in some can be more difficult than to indulge in none as the power of temptation thrives in scarcities and longings. Such a challenge is to be expected in return for the small pleasure in a life. Everything good and fun in life seems to come with price tags, and life is never fair to grant you anything for free. Self-control, at the very least, helps you steer away from either excess or absence and stay in the middle road safely.

Moderation and Balance

Moderation, or balance, is also the key to longevity. Everyone should have a long, healthy life despite the inevitability of diseases, toxins, and accidents threatening our lives all the time. In fact, one may question the need for self-control as it only takes a chance accident or a bad luck to take a life away and along with it all the efforts and moderation practiced so far to ensure a good, long life. Such a perspective renders any effort and activity in life meaning-less, however. It does alert us that life is short and unpredictable, and having fun while we can whatever we can may not seem like a bad idea altogether. Hence, the argument for self-control is mitigated to a suggestion at moderation and balance. Life is a cyclic process of good after bad, tragedies after comedies. To shun away the pleasures and fun thrown at your way adamantly is not only difficult but impossible at times. Instead of resisting pleasures outright, sometimes we have to accept and indulge in preparation for the uncertain tomorrow and doubtful future. Alcohol, smoking, and gambling are some of the things that can ruin your life in excess but can also make your life a little more interesting and fun with moderation and discipline. Many of us are already aware of such an inevitable law and are practicing hedonism and ascetic-ism from day-to-day basis. One day we live as if there is no tomorrow, and by the next day we regret having even thought of such a thing. We swear to drink ourselves to death and by the next morning we wish we died last night in existential pain and intestinal agony. We gamble away our money, time, and emotions on the silliest things such as a weekend at Vegas or an ill-fated partner perhaps way too often and frequently, but the important thing is we find balance in all of those things after failing and repeating. To fail and learn is life in a nutshell, and you live in a cycle and a pendulum of a life that always centers itself with time and practice. As long as you do not give up, balance finds you and molds to live with moderation and self-control. It is up to you, however, to make such a journey an easy and a painless one by understanding and starting fast and soon.

The Lifelong Process of Self-Control

Self-control is a constant, lifelong war you fight against your weaker, wanton self. You want to come out of each and every battle as the winner and the one in control. If the word 'fight' does not sound welcoming and fitting, try to think of it as a game or a competition you play against yourself. The game's goal is to resist temptations and even practice moderation while the ultimate prize the sense of pride and accomplishment for having become that much better as a person. Despite sounding cheesy, gamification of life's little and every aspect is a project that I am working on at the moment, and I strongly believe that competition and reward mechanism can improve a person and his or her overall life quality. That is, of course, as long as one is determined and sensible enough to want to better the self, and such determination and awareness require some degree of self-control practiced and exerted by default. Self-control in this context means more than just restraint and moderation; it means one's ability and the capability to take control of life.

Strict on the Self, Tolerant of the Others

One problem of this world is that many people are strict on others while far too lenient on themselves. If such a tendency were reversed, the world would have been a much better place than it is right now. Understanding and forgiving others' for their mistakes willingly and easily while putting ourselves to higher standards is the hallmark of advanced and peaceful humanity. While such a world sounds unfeasible and impossible at first thought, it is not as difficult as to achieve the world of forgiveness and understanding. People do not have to be understanding and self-controlled simultaneously. Practicing self-control naturally leads to better understanding and looser leniency on others because through self-control one is aware of how difficult and challenging it is to be so all the time. At the very least, there will be no one who is oxymoronically being strict on others while letting himself or herself get away with things easily. Whether people are strict on everyone including themselves or strict on themselves but not on others, either version of humanity is an upgrade to what we have right now.

22 SELF-LOVE

Love Yourself No Matter What

How much do you love yourself? If that
question sounds odd to you, then let me ask
you, instead, whether you love yourself or not.
The answers to such questions come in three
ways: yes, no, and 'why.' Why is loving one's
self necessary, one may wonder. Is loving one's
self a sign of sickly narcissism after all? There
is indeed something unfamiliar, embarrassing,
and rather vain about loving yourself, let alone
proudly claiming to do so. Should love towards
others be prioritized before selfishly loving
one's self? Therefore, the aforementioned
inquisitive answer to my seemingly rhetoric
question of whether you love yourself or not
comes to exist: is it necessary, or even okay, to

love yourself when there are other more pressing, public recipients of love present?

Yet only those who love themselves can fully and truly love others. We are rarely patient and logical in our ways of thinking and doing things in life, so most of us commit the mistake of rushing outside to find and exploit love rather than letting love flow from the inside. The consequence of neglecting love of the self and projecting it to appear in and to be taken away from others is often catastrophic. People who do not love themselves turn to others to fill the missing love in themselves, often resulting in lopsided relationships tainted with obsession and persistence. Such is the norm in the human affairs, and the problem lies in the fact that most people lack self-love throughout their lives. Rarely is taught the importance of self-love in contrast with love thy neighbors and thy gods, and rarely do we recognize the deficiency of love for ourselves until the said need becomes twisted desires and cravings that hurt not only ourselves but those around us.

It Is Okay to Be Selfish

You can, if not must, be a little selfish in order to love yourself. When it comes to choosing between loving yourself and sacrificing yourself for others, choose the former and never look back. The chances are that you, like most people in this world, are not a hero. The real heroes in life—the firefighters, police officers, soldiers, and even responsible parents—are able to sacrifice their lives for the greater good of other people because they believe in and love the ideals of their jobs, the values that their actions and possible sacrifices entail. The heroes themselves most likely do not even consider themselves as heroes, let alone sacrificial martyrs. The love of their vocations and duties, of what they do and what they represent, is a form of self-love and the secret behind the venerable superpowers they possess. Even the most admirably selfless people live with self-love and self-respect for themselves. The less heroic and more average people like you and me can simply follow suit and try the heroes' ways of life without the scary part about sacrificing own lives. That is, if you have and can instill self-love that you can believe in and sustain for life.

The Most Important Person in the Universe

You are the most important person in this universe. Not your friends, not your lovers, and not even your family. Remember they exist only because you exist. They may be your reasons for living and wanting to keep living, but the fact that they can only help you live and not actually live your life in your place. My suggestion to straighten the priority and hierarchy of love is to think to yourself that you are loving yourself who is loving those around you. Broaden and envelop the love all within you. Turn yourself into a spacious, capable nucleus of love. Think of love as an organic matter that can be birthed and grow. Then house that love, securely and warmly, in your heart that it never dies or goes away.

Love Yourself to Enable Yourself

By loving yourself foremost, you are able to do more things better and happier. For a starter, self-love gives you confidence. When you are confident, you feel invincible. Even when things go bad, you never take them as going bad. Mistakes become lessons, every surprise is a pleasant one, and there always seem to be a brighter tomorrow and an exciting next time. Self-love also grants comfort and peace inside you that no other person can give to you, not to mention the feeling of being in control all the time. You forgive more easily to yourself as well as others when you are at peace with yourself. Even in relationships with other people, the alternative to self-love is just a disastrous dependence and caustic clinging onto the other party. In short, you are as complete as you can be when you love yourself. When we try to do things and meet people without self-love, we are facing challenges and expecting the missing pieces from others as an incomplete, faulty people. We are imperfect however hard we try to be otherwise, but loving yourself is the closest we can reach to being complete and resilient, like a tilting doll that rises again after a fall thanks to the inherent balance in itself.

What Self-Love Looks Like

Self-love has many forms. If you are opposed to indulging yourself too much out of love, you can always be strict with yourself in a tough loving way. You do not have to publicly claim to be loving yourself if such a proclamation embarrasses you. It will be embarrassing for other people listening in as well. Self-love is a solitary, private undertaking, a life-long project and an unending, unforeseeable exploration. The only party involved is you and you only. Besides, never let others distract from your endeavor to endear yourself to you. You are both the subject and the object of this enduring mission. Be absolutely focused when it comes to finding what you love, hate, want, and fear. Be absurdly selfish when it comes to realizing those loves and wants and slaying those hates and fears. Love the fact that you are loving yourself and becoming better at it each day. Keep at it, and keep improving yourself and your life.

23 SOLITUDE

The Misunderstood Solitude

Solitude grants you the time to interact with yourself and yourself only. We are accustomed to spending time with others while feeling vulnerable and nervous when left alone because the society as a whole has encouraged people to interact with one another for centuries and even longer if we date the trend back to the Stone Ages and further. Thanks to our preference and tendency to stick together and avoid being solitary, we are conveniently and readily labeled the 'social animals,' while some of us are innately unsocial and do not like to be called animals in any occasion. Whereas the society benefits from a cohesive, intimate group of people forming a network or a community of markets, information, and public services in the name of civilization and urbanization, individuals enjoy the same benefits for freedom, personal space, and beauty of unpolluted, untainted nature. In order to reap the full benefits and gifts of this world, we have to implement both sociability and solitariness in our lives. Only through solitude can we discover who we really are, what we like and hate, as well as time and energy saved for the truly selfish, self-centered activities and deeds.

What It Means to Be Alone

You do not have to be alone all the time, nor can you truly be. Unless we seek out to isolate ourselves and live in the woods or an island, we will always be surrounded by people, both loving and hating. Company is the default state of being and living in most of today's urbanized, globalized residential settings. Company and social interaction are important, of course, but taking some time and personal space away from the constant congregation is equally important and yet considerably overlooked. In fact, those who favor solitude and isolation are deemed as abnormal, even unhealthy in some cultures. Being sociable is not the norm despite appearing to be so not because the majority of people are sociable and gregarious but because such people are more conspicuous and noticeable than their quieter, secluded counterparts. Even if there are more extroverted people out there than the introverts, there is no need for judgment or prejudice when it comes to personal preference and innate personality. Besides, the entire argument surrounding solitude is not that people should respect it as a personal choice, but rather that everyone should try to be solitary even sporadically to lead a better life and to become a better person. We all know the importance and benefits of being in company but only a few of us know and enjoy the benefits from being sociable as well as solitary. My suggestion is not to choose one or the other, but rather both of company and solitude.

How to Utilize Solitude

If the phrase 'being alone' makes you feel uncomfortable, try to see solitude as a time for recovery, meditation, and reflection. Because solitude is exactly that: the time and opportunity to provide for you the said activities and rest. If you are not a natural loner who actually likes the peace and quietness of solitude, you will have to force yourself into such a situation and circumstance. There are indeed people who just cannot stand being alone and staying home by themselves. They are often the same people who deem relaxing at home as 'doing nothing' or 'not busy at all' and activities that involve other people as only worthwhile and meaningful deeds of life. Just as they find introverted people who prefer staying home to going out pitiful and pathetic, the solitary introverts equally find those extroverts—who are, more often than not, loud, crass, and rude thanks to their supposedly superior preference of attending parties to reading books—missing out on the opportunity to spend time with the most important person in everyone's life universally and invariably: the self.

Solitude Is a Special Treat

Only the independent, thoughtful people can withstand periods of solitude. On the other hand, it may be that solitude turns people into independent, thoughtful beings through all the meditation and reflection performed meanwhile. The chicken or the egg debate aside, as long as one is capable of having solitary moments here and there to organize thoughts and look back on the self, solitude can serve as a meaningful ritual and practice to better the self.

Stress Is Other People

"Hell is other people," said Sartre, and the

brilliant man was correct. Most of the stress we incur from life come from being around other people. Even the most personal feelings, such as lack of confidence and low self-esteem, arise from comparing yourself to others in relatively, seemingly better states that you are in at the moment. Unfortunately, we can never be free from people. We live amongst them and also thanks to them. The basic necessities of life, including food, medical services, and air conditioning, are only available to us through the presence and efforts of farmers, doctors, and engineers, respectively. One may try to, and may succeed to, become a farmer who is a doctor and also an engineer at the same time, but such an attempt is almost impossible, let alone highly inefficient. Life is short, and we use help when help is around. Nevertheless, we should not be overly dependent on others. We have to be balanced between our dependence and independence, between company and solitude. Take only the absolutely crucial and beneficial provisions from the society while maintaining a peaceful, self-sufficient personal space and time for yourself. Too much of anything is as bad as too little of it. One who looks to company while neglecting the self will have nowhere else to take shelter once hurt and betrayed by others. The egotist who only cares about the self, too, will live with loneliness and inconvenience throughout life. Hence, a balanced life of social interaction and solitary deliberation is the optimal life one can have. Yet with the way people are more naturally inclined to be with one another, being actively and willfully solitary deserves an attention from those who wish for balanced lives, balanced selves.

24 SOPHISTICATION

What It Means to Be Sophisticated

To be sophisticated is to have a good taste. Despite sounding satisfactorily simple, this statement is as broad as a description can be. The question that is inevitably evoked is, then, "Who determines a 'good taste' and in what exactly?" To be fair, the word 'sophistication' should not scare you as it is just, merely, a word that sounds heavier than its substance. A good taste, on the other hand, is trickier because the standards of good tastes in this world are both subjective and objective, not to mention changing from time to time, back and forth. For example, reading a novel at the end of the day with a brandy and cigar may sound like what heaven looks like for some people while it strikes as phony and debaucherous for

others. Such differences in preferences cannot
be corrected but only be respected.

Going back to the supposed shallowness of the
word 'sophistication,' It is not the definition on
paper but rather the effort and practice
involved in the process within the real life that
attributes to the word's intimidation and
gravity. Whereas the word 'sophistication' is as
empty as the heads of those who try to pretend
that they possess it, the practice of sophistication dispenses with the stigma of vanity and
shallowness altogether. The practice of sophistication, naturally, is difficult and often a
constant, lifelong process. It is up to you, of
course, to make the process enjoyable or
unbearable on top of being difficult and lasting.

The Importance of Education

Sophistication comes through education. Education means more than just schooling in this
context, however. Training is also a form of
education. Any action that broadens your
knowledge and improves your skills is an act of
sophistication. Education and learning can
continue throughout your life as long as you
are willing to put yourself to the challenge.
From archaeology to zoology, the academia has
more than plenty of subjects for you to pursue

and contribute to the humanity by accumulating knowledge and experiments. Studying is not limited only to academics either. From archery s to zip-lining, hobbies and leisurely activities can also be studied and refined to hone your skills and expertise.

The More You Know, the More You See

The more you know, the more you can see and enjoy life. An adept skier sees a mountain and plans a downhill course while an avid hiker sees a thrilling adventure ahead in the same mountain. A painter, a poet, and a paleontologist—yes, you read correctly as he is the one who searches for dinosaur fossils—join the crew and set about what fun they all have in their minds. Meanwhile, an average Joe looks at the mountain and thinks, "Why bother?" Joe is not dumb or rude; he just does not see as the rest of them.

The Eternal Sophistication

There is no end to sophistication. Like a knife or a sword that can be made sharper with each honing, your acumen and competence can only grow bigger and brighter with each knowledge and practice. There is also no limitation or conformity to sophistication. An automobile mechanic who turns a carcass of a car into a functioning one is an artist in his or her own way. A surgeon who performs a high-end, intricate brain surgery of the first of its kind is both a life-saver and a a pioneer of the field of medicine and of neurology. You do not have to be a doctor, astronaut, or an engineer to be sophisticated beyond limitations. Sure, such professions may have a higher chance of impacting the world and the history given that the said occupation holders are more intelligent and driven than most people in the first place. But anyone can break the boundaries of his or her own world through being sophisticated in his or her own small and personal ways. Reading a book so not only that you become more knowledgeable but also that your children mimic you and develop a habit of reading is a great impact of its own. Learning about the environmental dangers and stopping yourself from using pollution-inducing products is also a small but meaningful way of letting your sophistication affect the world in a positive way.

Sophistication for the Self

Sophistication is not for show but for the self. The admiration from others and impacting the world are only accessories to how much you enjoy and benefit from being sophisticated.

Forget impressing those around you by flaunting your knowledge and showing off your skills. Forget how your act will lead to the betterment of the world, at least not yet. Instead, immerse yourself into whatever you are doing at the moment to learn, train, and simply do for the sake of learning, training, and doing. Let the flow of concentration and deliberation engulf you and trap you in the moment and the moment only. Sophistication is not only for pleasure but should be a pleasant process itself. In other words, you should not force yourself to learn and train to do things that you do not like and rather make you miserable. Schools are unpopular because they try to teach you everything instead of only the things that you like. On the other hand, colleges and universities are generally much more fun and liberating because students can now choose which subjects and courses to learn and take. Mandatory education is important so far in that it enables you to recognize your taste and preferences, more so than making you memorize the Boyle's law or the equation of an asymptote that you will hardly have to use in an ordinary circumstance.

If learning anything displeases you and you choose to be unsophisticated throughout your life, that is fine too. You have made a decision based on your wants and preferences, and you will try your best to retain the status quo of non-learning and non-forcing. I would say that is a sophistication of its own, with a hint of nihilism, à la Diogenes.

25 VISION

Time and Again

Time is fair, sometimes fiercely so, and the past always leaves and the future inevitably comes to us regardless of our say in the matter. Most people understand this natural phenomenon quite naturally with time and experience, but only a few perceive time's fluidity with a sense of urgency while the majority just accept it with nonchalance and resignation. As popular sayings go, bygones be bygones, and whatever will be, will be. One who dreads coming future does not deserve one. The worse kind, however, is the one that does not care whether future comes or not. Such a person lives as if there is no tomorrow not because he or she lives in the moment of the present but because of either laziness or fatigue, and even when tomorrow indeed comes lives on the same boring, lethargic existence. Time may be fair but life is not, and when life is teeming with problems from the past and of now, the future has to wait, get in a line before it gets its turn for hoarding attention and energy spent on then and now. Yet future never waits and storms upon us at one point or another. When it comes to facing the future, we are the one who should wait and prepare. Time is not our ally, but whether it becomes our enemy or a neutral party to our cause can be determined only through our action and understanding of our limited capabilities in dealing with time.

The Blueprint for the Future

Envision yourself in a year, five years, and a decade from now if you are not already doing so. It is easy to get lost in time as you get older, not to mention forget how old you are or how old you will be in five years from now. The older you get, the less exciting you are about birthdays and the New Year's Day. We either forget or try to forget that we are aging and nearing death while leaving the fun and the fresh experience of the youth farther behind the irretrievable past. As a result, it is easy to just go with the flow and age mindlessly, straying not too far away from the comfortable status quo and changing as little as possible. Besides, once you become an adult, there is not much room for change as was there when you were younger. Responsibilities, habits, preferences, health, vitality, and the likes have long shaped and shackled you from deviating from the stable, safe norm of the present. Yet despite the seemingly comfortable and convenient now and the continuous flow of immutability stemming from the present, we have to change and take control of where we are going. Stagnation, albeit not the worst, is far from the best situation in which you should shelter yourself. We should always strive to change ourselves for the better, and even maintaining the happiness and stability of the current timeline requires efforts and sacrifices. We have to consistently keep watch of where we are going and what we are becoming either to ensure a better future or a continuation of the best present. You may think that you will stay the same person you are in five or ten years from now with relative ease but future is unpredictable as it is uncontrollable. People change more so because situations call for changes rather than because they want to. Looking ahead to what will happen and keeping track of where you are headed is a crucial part to readying yourself against the future as well as being macroscopic in both temporal and spatial aspects. In its core is the ability and the willingness to imagine yourself and direct yourself to the desired destination, and that is what envisioning is all about.

Visualizing Your Future

You need to more than just prepare for the future; you need to see yourself in it. In two of the prior entries in this essay series, I have discussed the importance of being ready for anything that will happen to you and also of being macroscopic in viewing the world and the time. Whereas readiness and macroscopism are of being actively prepared for both the present and future exigencies and of having a broader perspective in general, respectively, vision is specifically about 'seeing' the future in an imaginative, constructive way. Think of it as drawing a mental map that outlines the courses and the destinations of your life at certain critical points. What will you be doing when you are thirty? Whom will you be with on your fortieth birthday? What kind of parent will you be like? How much loving of a grandparent? We have all imagined ourselves to be someones else at some point in our lives, and more often have we pictured our perfect futures and dreams. We may not live out our dreams 100% accurately and literally, but once we have seen what our futures can look like, we now have a blueprint of the best future that is possible. All you have to do from then is to try to make it real, and sometimes that makes all the difference.

Living Your Life Thrice

Life is both short and long, depending on how you use your time. If you let time pass away mindlessly and carelessly, life will indeed feel short and empty. On the other hand, spending every minute diligently and crisply according to the plan as well as reliving the past and envisioning the future back and forth will make you feel as if you are living two or three simultaneous lives at the same time. You live once by living the present, twice by remembering the past, and thrice by planning the future.

Dreams, Visions, and Realities

'Vision' is just another word for 'dream.' At the same time, a vision is more concrete and objective than a dream. To dream denotes to wish and to hope, not without a hint of fantasy and optimism, while to envision is to simulate and imagine yourself in a probable and likely situation in the future. Try to be visionaries rather than just dreamers. You can always start with a dream, but make sure to solidify your future with a vision. Vision, I strongly believe, turns a dream into a reality.

ABOUT THE AUTHOR

Sage Egerton is a social theorist and engineer who writes essays and books that help people improve their lives and make this world an overall better place to live. You can also search the web for his pen-name 'Solitary Essayist' for more writings and theories about life, society, relationships, and history.

Made in the USA
Columbia, SC
07 December 2024